Living a Transformed Life

"Wow, this book hits it dead on. It starts with correcting the false view of God and Jesus' purpose and plan and ends with affirming what the Word of God shows us as truth and how to live it. It's not very often I read a book, especially a Christian one, and I am so completely touched. I know I need to meditate on this and let it soak in."

—**LYDIA SWALCHICK**, ACT Conference Coordinator

"*Living a Transformed Life* is a must-read for anyone interested in deepening their faith or desiring a closer walk with Jesus. In the book, Paul Feider describes the key elements of transformation and how they progress from the head to the heart. There are abundant and well documented scripture references as well as emphasis on the power of the Holy Spirit in spiritual transformation. I plan to incorporate this text into our discipleship training program."

—**MIKE SABBACK**, convener, South Carolina OSL (Order of St. Luke) Healing Community

"This book captures Paul Feider's love for Jesus and his profound knowledge of the Scriptures. It answered all my questions about Christianity and ignited a fire in me to live this transformed life in the power of the Holy Spirit. I now understand what it means to have a personal relationship with Jesus and the peace flowing from that relationship. This book will captivate your heart and refresh your mind. It has transformed me."

—**KEN KURTENACKER**, disciple

"Paul Feider has a remarkable gift of describing key bedrock Scriptures with profound clarity and simplicity. Paul passionately invites us to move deeper into our own Spirit-led faith journey, where 'instead of seeking worldly pleasure and power, we experience the deep joy of walking daily in God's will with Jesus walking beside us.' His chapters on the Spiritual Enrichment Retreat provides a simple yet profound way to enter into that deeper walk with Jesus. The questions at the end of each chapter will be a valuable resource for both individual and small group study."

—**JOHN RICE**, director, The Blessing
Place of Western North Carolina

"Who doesn't want to live a better, healthier, happier life!? Paul Feider takes the reader on a step-by-step walk on living a life as Jesus intended. It is all about choice. It is not always easy to follow the path our Lord has laid down. However, with each session in the book, with the questions at the end of each session, Father Paul leads you into a stronger understanding of Jesus and a transformation of our body, soul, and mind."

—**MALCOLM SELF**, former board member,
International Order of St. Luke the Physician

"In this book, Paul Feider has offered a path to a more meaningful and deeper spiritual life for those of us who wish to follow Jesus into a fuller relationship with the Father. He takes us through a series of spiritual exercises that help us restore our image of God. Paul is an excellent teacher, a sensitive pastor, and a spiritual director. This book can take any follower of Christ deeper in and higher up on our journey."

—**KEVIN MARTIN**, retired dean,
Cathedral Church of St. Matthew

"*Living a Transformed Life* is a book whose purpose is to help a person recognize their 'gift and call.' Fr. Paul Feider concentrates on specific areas to help you realize God's gifts to you and how to use them yourself and for others. This book specifically focuses on our present world and how to live a 'Jesus filled' life. When you see the world from this perspective, it can be life changing. Thank you Fr. Paul for once again using your 'gift and call' in the service of others."

—**VICKIE BAUCH**, convener, OSL (Order of St. Luke) St. Johns Healing Community

"Paul Feider has a gentle way of nudging us along in our relationship with God. By surrounding our will to God's will, Paul's writings open up the Holy Spirit to move and transform our ordinary lives into extraordinary. He has the unique capacity to combine deep scriptural truths with practical applications. By reading this book and providing space in your life to apply these truths, your soul will be fulfilled."

—**TODD A. McGREGOR**, clergy in residence, St. David's in the Pines

"Paul Feider's book offers a refreshing perspective on spirituality, emphasizing the direct personal encounter with God in the midst of ordinary life. Feider's recurrent theme of our brokenness resonates deeply, highlighting how our failure to live in accordance with Jesus' teachings stems from our own human brokenness. Yet, amidst this brokenness, Feider's compassion and sensitivity shine through, offering readers a path towards aligning with the reality of God's love through Jesus Christ. Whether read individually or within groups, Feider's work provides valuable insights and guidance for those seeking to deepen their spiritual journey."

—**JOSH ACTON**, North American director, Order of St. Luke the Physician

Living a Transformed Life

The Core of Christianity

PAUL FEIDER

RESOURCE *Publications* · Eugene, Oregon

LIVING A TRANSFORMED LIFE
The Core of Christianity

Resource Publications
An Imprint of Wipf and Stock Publishers
199 W. 8th Ave., Suite 3
Eugene, OR 97401

www.wipfandstock.com

PAPERBACK ISBN: 979-8-3852-2119-6
HARDCOVER ISBN: 979-8-3852-2120-2
EBOOK ISBN: 979-8-3852-2121-9

VERSION NUMBER 06/14/24

Thank you, Donna Self, Vickie Bauch, and Ken Kurtenacker
for helping make this book possible.

Contents

Introduction

"Do not conform yourselves to this age but be transformed by the renewal of your mind, so that you may judge what is God's will, what is good, pleasing and perfect"

ROMANS 12:2

These words written by the apostle Paul invite us to consider a more fulfilling way of living. They afford us a vision of a better life, the life God intended for us. They challenge us to step out of our natural inclinations of seeking only our own pleasure and discovering the immense pleasure of living in the divine Presence.

This book is about discovering the transformed life, the empowered life, the beautiful life, and then being equipped to live that life. It is about living the dream, God's dream for you. It is also a valuable tool for sharing the original understanding of Christianity with others and letting them know of the power available to those who follow Jesus. It is a journey into the "much greater" that is possible for anyone who wants more joy, serenity, and peace. Whether you have tasted this life and want more or have never heard of this life and desire to learn, this text will show you the way.

I have listened to many people who try to fill their longing for fulfillment by consuming things. They always come up short. They always want one more thing. Others spend enormous amounts of time sitting on the couch to be entertained by the television or computer, but end up feeling empty with no deeper goals or purpose. I have spoken with some who never spent the energy to develop their talents, and so they end up depressed. They often try to live out their life vicariously through some movie star, athlete, or even their children, yet they often feel empty inside. I see many people who are always hurried, staying busy with many activities, or surrounded by constant noise so they do not feel the pain that exists within.

The good news is that I have watched many of those people be transformed by the renewal of their hearts and minds. Through an openness to receive a flood of unconditional love and a readiness to begin a divine journey, they experience the greater life, the fuller life, the real joy in life. Their decision to be transformed opened their hearts to feel a love they never knew and opened their minds to want to learn about the God who created them. I have shared these teachings and spiritual treasures during almost fifty years of pastoring. In every situation, more people kept coming, wanting to experience the transforming power that was available to them.

I have walked with many people along this divine journey, which begins with a decision and eventually ends in a new way of viewing themselves, their relationships, and their Creator. They have a joy that is noticeable to others and a peace that pervades their whole being. In these following chapters, I will share some things that make this journey and the final goal possible. As we let divine love soak into our being and open our minds to a new divine worldview, we get morphed into a person living the fullness of life that Jesus desires.

This book portrays the beauty and serenity of life immersed in the awareness of God's Presence. It lays out the journey that leads to a life of deep joy, a meaningful life. I will describe some significant factors contributing to this kind of transformed life. We will look at Jesus' picture of God and walk through a series of reflections, allowing us to experience God's rich, transforming love. We will address the healing effects of God's Presence in our lives. Next, we will take an in-depth look at the bedrock scriptures that lay the foundation for authentic Christianity and a transformed life. Finally, we will consider other New Testament writings which inform us about Jesus and the first people who committed their life to him.

I invite you to relax and soak in the many scripture verses that express God's love for you. I encourage you to slowly digest the texts that show us a God of extravagant love and indescribable generosity. I invite you to receive all God wants to give to you as you seek a transformed life. This journey is a God-anointed one and it is for you.

CHAPTER 1

Transforming Our Picture of God

We do not exactly know what God is like. We each have our ideas. I enjoyed the story of the little boy who was drawing at the table while his mother made dinner. His mom asked him, "What are you drawing?" He answered, "I am drawing a picture of God." His mom said, "People don't know what God looks like." The boy responded, "They will when I get done!" Children sometimes have a better picture of God because they just came from God and have not had their picture distorted by others or the events in their lives. I remember one day when our friends came to our house with their family. We ended up playing hide and seek. I found one of the little girls in my office. As we stood there, I noticed my picture of Jesus on the wall. It was painted by a young girl who had a near-death experience and saw Jesus. When she came back to life, she painted this picture. I pointed out the picture to this little girl and asked her if she knew who that was. I knew she had no church background or any chance to know Jesus. She looked at the picture for a long time. Then she took two steps closer. Finally, she said, "It's Jesus." I asked how she knew. She said, "I looked into his eyes." She remembered what Jesus looked like. Jesus said, "Whoever has seen me, has seen the Father" (John 14:9).

You probably have heard the story of the little girl who lived with alcoholic parents. She never received much love or care. One night, when her dad came home drunk, he shot her mom and then shot himself. The little girl hid behind the couch as all of this went on. She was eventually taken to foster parents, who showed her love and gave her a chance to learn about God. When she first went to Sunday school, she saw a crucifix. She said to the teacher, "I don't know who that is on the cross, but I know he got off because he was there by me the night my mommy and daddy died." She knew Jesus. She had a clear picture of him. She experienced his love and protection.

To discover a clear picture of God, we need to read Jesus' words about God the Father and allow his message to dispel any distorted picture we may have lived with for quite a while. If we look at the oldest gospel, the gospel of Mark, we see that it contains the actual Aramaic words that Jesus spoke. It gives us the most authentic image of Jesus, his teachings, and his description of God. In Mark chapter 14, verse 36, we read how Jesus in the garden of Gethsemane prayed in his moment of deepest need. He said, "*Abba*, take this cup away from me, but not as I will but as you will." Jesus offered a new picture of God, which surprised even his followers. He called God *Abba*, the Aramaic word for "daddy." The Jews with whom he lived called God *Yahweh*, and they would not even say the name of God. Only once a year could the high priest do that. Their picture was of a distant God who created but also showed his wrath at times. Jesus, the incarnate Son of God, offered a picture of God who is personal, extravagantly loving, and desires to be close to each person. When the disciples asked Jesus to teach them to pray, he said, "When you pray, say '*Abba*,' Father hallowed be thy name. . ." This picture updates the Old Testament picture of God and can change any skewed picture of God we may have.

As I mentioned, this is a direct teaching from Jesus. Some people get distracted by Jesus calling God *Abba* or Father because it is a male image. If a male figure has hurt them or they never had a good experience with their father, this can be a challenge. Often, I have seen people healed from their lack of a good father figure or the wounds that males inflicted by experiencing *Abba's* love. They learn what a father's love is supposed to feel like. *Abba's* love filled in the emptiness they had felt because they lack a good father. I have found that many people carry a father wound and many have been healed of it by taking time to receive the perfect love of *Abba*.

Let me also add that in the Bible, Wisdom, which is somewhat like the Holy Spirit, was always referred to with feminine pronouns, meaning that we could experience the Holy Spirit as the feminine dimension of God. Jesus gives us a picture of God as a community of love—*Abba*, Jesus, and the Holy Spirit. This picture of God is more relational than the description of God as *Yahweh* in the Old Testament. Accepting and internalizing Jesus' picture of God often brings healing to people's father wounds and mother wounds as well as their emotional hurts. This description of God as Father, Son, and Holy Spirit is perhaps Jesus' greatest gift to humanity, and it is found in our bedrock scriptures.

Our skewed picture of God can block our chance of experiencing *Abba* or the Holy Spirit and make it difficult to go through life without feeling God's unconditional love. I read a book by an atheist. He described his picture of God as being shaming, judgmental, and only interested in blaming us for our sins. He got his picture from his church, where the pastor and Sunday School teacher apparently had a distorted picture of God. He didn't believe in a God like that. I wouldn't either. Instead of discovering the God revealed by Jesus in the gospels, he chose not to believe in God. It left him empty and devoid of the transformed life that would have been possible. I have spoken with numerous people like this who have never experienced God's perfect, unconditional love. When they took time to read Jesus' words and experience God's love, their lives were transformed. Jesus has drawn a beautiful picture of God, which is recorded in the gospels. God's love flows out from between the lines of those accounts.

I meet many people who have a distorted picture of God. Some have been abused and wonder why God did not stop the abuser. Their hurt is understandable. They feel that God does not care about human suffering. I explained to them that God could not stop the abuser. The abuser had free will. When God created free will, he gave humans the chance to choose a life with him and live with him forever, but it also gave humans the chance to turn away and do devastating things. It must pain God to see how humans hurt themselves and each other. God could have controlled every person's actions. God chose to make humans rather than robots. God chose intimacy over control. He did promise to stand with us in the difficult times in life. We saw this in the story of the little girl behind the couch. Jesus stood with her in her deepest need, and she knew it. The dad was free to shoot the mom and himself, but Jesus was there with the little girl. Jesus reveals a God who would die to forgive and heal the wounds caused by the misuse of human freedom. God absorbed the pain into himself so we could be redeemed and forgiven. That is an awesome gift. We can receive that healing and forgiving love as part of the transformed life.

It is important to note that suffering is not evidence against God. We can get a mistaken notion about God from the phrase we sometimes hear after a natural disaster or serious accident. People describe what occurred as "an act of God." A more accurate phrase is that it was "an act of evil." I believe that the tragedies and disruptions in the world are an accumulation of centuries of human sin and the power of evil connected to that sin. The gospels reveal a God who is perfect love, and perfect love would not do such things. Giving humans free will is a huge cost to God. Having God with us through the tragedies and the human inspiration to help one another, as Jesus taught, is a great benefit.

Some view God the Father as one who sends tragedies to get even with people. That does not fit with what Jesus revealed. God does not get revenge. Sometimes, humans paint their desire for revenge on God, but Jesus' picture of God does not match that kind of God. Some feel God sends sickness to teach people a lesson. A God of love would never do that. God could not do that. God would stop being God if he did not love with perfect love. God sent prophets, teachers, and his own Son, Jesus, to teach people how to live a transformed life. God would not think of sending sickness or tragedy for that purpose.

I work with many people who think God is against them because of an illness or the illness of someone they know. Jesus did not explain why suffering or illness happen, but when he met a sick or hurting person, he was "moved with compassion," and his deep love healed them. He revealed a God who cares very deeply for the well-being of each person.

Some feel God is punishing them by making them sick. Jesus' healing ministry clearly dispels that theory. Obviously, God the Father could not be in heaven sending sickness to punish people if his Son was on earth healing the sicknesses. That would be a fight in the Godhead. The gospels reveal that God is on the side of health and wholeness. A better explanation is that evil causes sickness. We also know that sometimes humans cause sickness or woundedness by not taking care of their body or dealing with their emotions. At times, humans abuse others physically or emotionally. There can be woundedness coming to us from our generational lines that makes us susceptible to illness. There can be many factors, but it is clear from the gospels that God does not cause sickness. What is sad is that if someone thinks that God made them sick, then they would not pray for healing. This theory diminished the healing ministry for centuries. The gospels tell us that God wants us to be well and that we can pray God's love into anyone who is sick to bring healing. When we pray for healing and invite the person to feel God's awesome, deep love for them, healing always happens on some level. Some are cured physically. Some experience a release from pain, and some feel a greater inner peace. Some experience a safe place to talk about deeper issues at the root of an illness which opens the way to healing. I have seen many people restored who receive healing prayer. It is one of the benefits of a transformed life.

Another benefit of seeking to get an accurate picture of God is that we feel a new identity and an increase in our self-esteem. We read in the gospel that Jesus was, "Fully aware that he had come from the Father, and was going back to the Father" (John 13:3). That was his identity and the source of his power to heal and forgive. Once we experience that we are sons and daughters of the Father, we can feel a similar identity. We then know whose sons and daughters we are. Our true identity comes from God. Discovering our true identity, receiving Jesus' transforming love, and living as he taught makes us his disciples. That deep connection to our Creator gives us an inner strength and confidence to face life. In the gospel, we see how the disciples of Jesus radically changed once they started following Jesus and listening to his teachings. He introduced them to the Father and the Holy Spirit, and their lives were never the same.

This new picture of God also takes away any fear of death. Once we experience ourselves as God's children, we can live in peace and die in peace. We recognize, like Jesus, that we came from the Father and are going back to the Father. Only if we are disconnected from God through our actions do we need to fear going back to the Father.

To let our picture of God be transformed, we need to decide to come and see. In the gospel of John, we read how John the Baptist encouraged his disciples to follow Jesus, which they did. It says, "When Jesus turned around and noticed them following him, he asked them, 'What are you looking for?' They said, 'Where do you stay?' He answered, 'Come and see'" (John 1:38–39). They asked a question, and he offered them an invitation. They had to come and see to discover the transformed life and a more accurate picture of God. The text does not give any directions to Jesus' house. It calls the disciples to a movement in their hearts and minds. They had to let go and leave the place where they "stayed" in their mind, their worldview, and their picture of God. They were invited to go beyond the place where they lived in their hearts to where they felt that there must be more to life. They were invited into the divine journey of transformation to discover the fullness of life, a life with rich joy and deep purpose. They were invited to walk with Jesus to feel his love and witness the miracles that flowed from his presence. They had to decide to enter the journey with Jesus and open their minds to the greater, fuller life of deep joy and peace.

Many others in the gospel were invited to "come and see" but were unwilling to let go of their old views and ways of filling their human longings. They chose to stay stuck in their ways and missed the transformed life that Jesus offered to them. We each have that same decision to make. To know real life, we must move away from our old views and open ourselves to God's view for our lives. We have to look closely at Jesus as revealed in the gospels and be open to seeing and experiencing his gentle heart of compassion and deep love. Jesus said, "Whoever has seen me, has seen the Father" (John 14:9). Looking closely at the life of Jesus changes our picture of God and allows us to experience unconditional love. In this next chapter, I invite you to "come and see."

Prayer to Know God

Father, Son, and Holy Spirit, reveal your Presence to me in a new way. Cleanse from my mind any distortions that I have about you and fill my mind and heart with a true image of who you are. Heal any part of me that keeps me from desiring to receive your love. Jesus, I thank you for giving me a clear picture of the Divine Presence and for allowing me to experience that Presence every day. Keep me surrounded in your divine love so that it will soak through my whole being and heal me of anything that is not of you. Thank you, Father, Son, and Holy Spirit, for creating me and being with me always. Amen.

Questions

What is your picture of God? Are you open to changing it, to make it more scriptural, and more like Jesus taught?

What experiences in your life may have colored your picture of God?

Are you open to a deeper experience of God?

Chapter 2

The Spiritual Enrichment Retreat

We have taken time to examine our picture of God and perhaps update it according to what Jesus said. In this chapter, we will look at many scripture passages that draw us into feeling God's love for us. We will take time to move from our head knowledge to a profound heart experience. This chapter is designed to be used as a six-week retreat, which has been very helpful in opening thousands of people to a personal encounter with the heart of God. It is a set of reflections and scripture readings that offer the opportunity to discover the transformed life. I have witnessed many people's lives transformed as they journeyed through this retreat. I would gather people who wanted to "come and see" who Jesus is and spend six weeks walking with him. You can make this retreat yourself, but inviting one or more people to walk it with you might be a richer experience. Even if you have reflected on these scriptures before, the words take on deeper meaning as you grow spiritually.

I begin each session with prayer and a teaching and then break into small groups to share what God is saying to each person. Then, I instruct each participant to take at least 15 minutes of quiet time each day and use the following scriptures and reflections to enter into a heart conversation with Jesus. During these times, people often felt Jesus' care for them and the Father's deep love for them. For the following week, we gather to share what God has revealed to them during the week in their quiet time and then continue with the next theme.

If you do not have time to do the retreat now, you might read through the reflections, absorbing them as you go. When you have more time, you can come back and walk through this retreat over six weeks, allowing the words to soak deeper into your being. Sharing what you experience with another person can solidify it in your heart and bring about a lasting transformation.

Following are summaries of the teachings as well as the scriptures and reflections.

This retreat fulfills God's promise, *"To anyone who thirsts I will give to drink without cost from the spring of life-giving water. . ."* (Revelations 21:6)

This promise is for every person, and it is for you. It is for you who want something more; for you who know that you have a thirst which has not yet been satisfied; for you who have heard of a "water" that refreshes beyond compare; for you who are wounded who are aching to be loved into wholeness; for you who are on top of the world, but know that all the world does not have enough to sustain real life; for you who are full of fears and yet long for true peace. For you who want all a human being can have, for all people, there is this promise made by God, who created you.

Maybe you have known God all your life but are wondering how to feel God's nurturing love. Maybe you are searching for God but struggling with how to talk with the One who created you. Now, God speaks to you. Now, God offers you a promise, a free gift, a new life—without a price because God loves you. *"Let the one who is thirsty come forward; let all who desire it accept the gift of life-giving water"* (Revelation 22:17).

If your experience of religion has not been fulfilling, if you go to church but nothing seems to change, or if you have stopped going altogether, then this retreat is for you and the people about whom you care. It is an invitation to experience a re-awakening of your baptism, to experience a new energy, a fresh outpouring of the Holy Spirit. I invite you to take this opportunity to receive.

SESSION ONE—*GOD'S LOVE*

(Below is a summary of the session one teaching. Quiet yourself and receive it into your heart.)

Perhaps the greatest gift Jesus gave to his disciples and us is his picture of an intimate, loving God. The Jews had come to understand God as somewhat distant and judgmental. They were not even allowed to say the name of God. Growing up with this vision of God, we understand why the disciples must have been surprised when they asked Jesus to teach them to pray, and he said, "When you pray, say, '*Abba*, Father, who art in heaven. . .'" He taught them what we know as the Lord's Prayer. Jesus gave them a new picture of God. He let them know they could speak with God as a loving father who desired to be close to them. The gospel tells us that Jesus often went off alone to deepen that intimate relationship he had with *Abba* (Luke 5:16). That intimate love relationship sustained him in his moment of deepest sorrow and distress in the garden of Gethsemane just before he was crucified (Mark 14:36). This awareness of God's love would sustain the disciples after Jesus ascended into heaven.

God loves us very deeply. We may know this, but we want to take time to feel it this week. We will never experience God's deep love unless we allow ourselves to do so. We must open our hearts to being intimate with God, to share our feelings, and to listen to God's feelings for us. We take time this week to hear God express his love for us through the scripture readings.

God invites us personally into the Trinity—the Father, Jesus, and the Holy Spirit—all wrapping divine love around us. It is this perfect love in which we were conceived and which is available to us as we live a transformed life. Feeling this love gives us energy, an identity, and heals our wounds. It is the foundation of Christianity.

We may have grown up with some misconceptions of Christianity. We may think of Christianity as a set of restrictions only or that it is just a matter of doing this and not doing that. Christianity is, first of all, feeling loved by God. Because we feel so loved, we want to do what God desires. It is not so much doing as it is letting God's love empower us to do what is wholesome for us and our neighbors.

Perhaps we also think that God is too distant, or cannot be contacted, or is too busy for us. That simply is not true. God desires to contact us. God can be close to each of us at the same time. God wants to hold us close. We read in the prophet Hosea, "When Israel (we can put our name in here) was a child, I loved him, I called my son. The more I called them, the further they went from me sacrificing to idols. Yet it was I who taught them to walk, who took them in my arms; I drew them with human cords, with bands of love; I fostered them like one who raises an infant to his cheeks; yet though I stooped to feed my child, they did not know that I was their healer" (Hosea 11:1–4).

We can feel God directly loving us, even if someone in our past has damaged our picture of God or if we grew up with the idea that God was out to punish us. God continues to keep on loving us, no matter what. Through our reflection on the life and attitudes of Jesus, we can realize that God wants only the best for us and wants us happy and healthy. When we are not so, God is always at our side, trying to lead us to wholeness. God cannot, however, take away people's free will. People may have hurt us in the past and may still harm us. God cannot stop them, but he can protect and heal us with his extravagant love. God's love can empower us with the energy and security to journey toward greater wholeness and inner peace.

This direct experience of God leads to a new, transformed life, a new perspective of life. We begin to look at all life events and our relationships in light of God's intense love for us. It is a love that gives deep peace. This next week, we will take daily quiet time to receive this marvelous gift.

Questions

Have you ever felt God's love for you in a very intense way?

I there anything missing in your life? A longing or an emptiness? Would you like to have it filled?

We approach this retreat with expectancy, open to a new and deeper love relationship with God. Take *15 minutes of quiet time* every day this week and soak in the following scriptures and reflections. If you struggle with getting yourself quiet, I invite you to check out chapter three of my book, *Journey to Inner Peace*. It offers ways of quieting out hearts and minds and readying ourselves to hear God.

Day 1

Jesus introduced us to God and called God *Abba*. He wanted us to know we could be close to God and feel his gentle love. God said, "With age-old love I have loved you; so I have kept my mercy toward you" (Jeremiah 31:3).

Day 2

God formed the people of Israel and formed each of us as his own. We read, "Thus says the Lord who created you, and formed you Israel, 'Fear not, for I have redeemed you; I have called you by name; you are mine'" (Isaiah 43:1).

Day 3

God, who created the universe and has kept it in order, has personal time to spend with you and desires to do so. God cares deeply for you. God promised, "I myself will pasture my sheep; I myself will give them rest, says the Lord God. The lost I will seek out, the strayed I will bring back, the injured I will bind up, the sick I will heal, shepherding them rightly" (Ezekiel 34:15–16).

Day 4

Because God loves us, he sent his Son to save us. He sent Jesus so we might have the fullness of life now and a life that will last forever. We read, "Yes, God so loved the world that he gave his only Son that whoever believes in him may not die, but may have eternal life" (John 3:16).

Day 5

God loves you and invites you to drink in all the love he has for you. God is saying to you, "All you who are thirsty, come to the water. You who have no money, come, receive grain and eat; come without paying and without cost, drink wine and milk. Why spend your money for what is not bread; your wages for what fails to satisfy? Heed me, and you shall eat well, you shall delight in rich fare. Come to me heedfully, listen that you may have life" (Isaiah 55:1–3).

Day 6

If you wish to share a deeper life with God, turn to him, seek him with all your heart and spend time talking with him. God says to you, "I know well the plans I have in mind for you, says the Lord, plans for your welfare, not for woe, plans to give you a future full of hope. When you call me, when you go to pray to me, I will listen to you. When you look for me, you will find me. Yes, when you seek me with all your heart, you will find me with you, says the Lord, and I will change your lot" (Jeremiah 29:11–13).

Day 7

When God seems far away, or you do not know what to say, slowly reflect on the prayer Jesus taught us. Remember the gift Jesus gave us when he said you could call God, *Abba.* He said, "When you pray, say: '*Abba*,' Father, hallowed be your name, your kingdom come. Give us each day our daily bread. Forgive us our sins for we too forgive all who do us wrong; and subject us not to the trial" (Luke 11:2–4).

Other scriptures you might wish to read this week are John 1, John 14, and Colossians 1.

SESSION TWO—*THE GIFT OF SALVATION*

> (Below is a summary of the teaching for session two.
> Quiet yourself and receive it into your heart.)

We are seeking to experience *Abba*'s direct and living Presence, to feel his transforming love for us. We must come with expectant faith. We might begin by examining what has hampered our hearts from knowing God and feeling his deep love for us. We sense that there is something out of order in the world. Humans are good but have fallen. Sin has entered the world. We live in a sin-filled environment. There is a pervasive power of evil and sin evident around us. We know of wars, violence, injustice, and abuse. There are the sins of generations before us which affect our behavior and health. This collective sin is stronger than any human being can handle alone. These things all disrupt our inner peace and weigh on our spirit.

Then, we have our human feelings of grief, depression, anxiety, insecurity, fear, and anger. We may have experienced serious trauma in life and carry unresolved issues within our hearts. Counseling can help to some extent, but feeling God's deep love heals the core issues and allows us to live a life of freedom and serenity. We can feel a new identity as daughters and sons of *Abba*, which empowers us to experience deep, inner healing.

We need God to find the fullness of life. We need the awareness of God's love for us to resist temptations and not be swept up in the power of evil, which is often masked by "it's all right, everyone does it" or "just forget about it." We need to be transformed in our hearts and minds. We know that Christianity is no longer sustained by a universal Christian culture. Our culture and society often promote non-Christian values. To have the fullness of life, we cannot conform to our culture's values.

Human efforts to improve the world often aim at solving external problems using control, strength, science, pills, distractions, and cover-ups. God's love allows us to look within ourselves with new eyes to perceive the real, core problems, which may be selfishness, greed, dishonesty, or apathy. God's love gives us the inner security to face ourselves honestly and the inner strength to correct the behaviors that need to change. This is the gift of salvation.

We may experience the pain of changing, but we need not get buried in guilt. Jesus' love can forgive our past sins and heal our wounds. Once we choose to turn away from destructive patterns and seek forgiveness, God is ready to forgive. That gift was won for us by Jesus on the cross.

Human beings were created to need God to achieve true peace. Full humanity can only happen in union with God. Spirituality is not optional. Jesus said, "Apart from me you can do nothing" (John 15:5). We find healing, forgiveness, and wholeness only in God. God came into the world as Jesus to save us and free us from the world of sin. When we listen to him and choose to follow his will for us, we become truly free. "Do not be conformed to this world, but be transformed by the renewal of your mind, so that you may judge what is God's will, what is good, pleasing and perfect" (Romans 12:2).

The gift of salvation is not just heaven; it is a new way of life on earth, a life open to God's voice and love, a transformed life. This gift cannot be forced on anyone but needs a person's free inner decision. We must choose to let God direct our life. Imagine a two-seater bicycle. For some or most of our lives, Jesus has probably been on the back seat of our tandem bike as a helper we call upon when we need something. Jesus desires to sit on the front seat and steer our life. We must invite Jesus to sit on the front seat. It may seem scary to let go of control and let Jesus steer, but he knows which direction is best for our life. We must let him guide our lives and listen to his direction each day. We use our energy, but we use it to go where he wants us to go. That is true surrender, which brings great inner peace and serenity. Jesus knows the purpose of our life much better than we do. We only need to trust his voice. I invite you this week to make a choice to surrender completely to God and receive the joy of a new way of living life.

Questions

In what ways have you begun to feel God's love during these reflections?

What situations in our world or in your life make you aware of the need for God?

How do you feel about letting Jesus direct your life?

Take *15 minutes of quiet time* every day this week and soak in the following scriptures and reflections.

Day 1

God's vision for our wholeness and happiness is much bigger than the world can give. Human plans and philosophies are presented to us as the hope of the world, the ways of true happiness. God says, "As high as the heavens are above the earth, so high are my ways above your ways and my thoughts above your thoughts" (Isaiah 55:9).

Day 2

God wants us to feel his love, but sometimes, the world in which we live clouds our view and keeps us from knowing God's deep love. God invites us to pull away and listen. "In the days to come all nations shall stream toward the mountain of the Lord. Many peoples shall come and say, 'Come, let us climb the Lord's mountain, to the house of the God of Jacob, that he may instruct us in his ways, and we may walk in his paths'" (Isaiah 2:2–4).

Day 3

We need more than human ideas and human power to find real life and lasting peace. We need the wisdom and the power of God. We are facing a power that is greater than human power. Behind the world's evils is the power of the Evil one. The apostle Paul writes, "Our battle is not against human forces but against the principalities and powers, the rulers of this world of darkness, the evil spirits in regions above" (Ephesians 6:12).

Day 4

The Father sent Jesus into the world to save us, to free us from the power of the devil and the world so that we might live a new life now and enter final salvation forever in heaven. Paul explains, "You were dead because of your sins and offenses, as you gave allegiance to the present age. . . But God is rich in mercy; because of his great love for us, he brought us to life with Jesus Christ when we were dead in sin. By this favor you were saved" (Ephesians 2:1–5).

Day 5

Jesus died on the cross so that we might live in the freedom of his love. Paul says, "It is rare that anyone should lay down his life for a just man, though it is barely possible that for a good man someone might have the courage to die. It is precisely in this that God proves his love for us; that while we were still sinners, Christ died for us" (Romans 5:6–8).

Day 6

Jesus died and rose from the dead so we might have the gift of salvation. We read from Isaiah, "Yet it was our infirmities that he bore, our sufferings that he endured. While we thought of him as stricken, as one smitten by God and afflicted, but he was pierced for our offenses, crushed for our sins; upon him was the chastisement that makes us whole, by his stripes we were healed" (Isaiah 53:4–6).

Day 7

We must let go of our old securities to experience the freedom of salvation in Jesus. We read, "He rescued us from the power of darkness and brought us into the kingdom of his beloved Son. Through him we have redemption and the forgiveness of our sins" (Colossians 1:13–14).

Other scriptures you might wish to read this week are John 3, Ephesians 1, and 1 Corinthians 12.

SESSION THREE—*THE NEW LIFE IN JESUS*

(Below is a summary of the teaching for session three.
Quiet yourself and receive it into your heart.)

As you proceed through this retreat, you may notice that your prayer is changing. You may want to talk with God more intimately. I encourage you to try conversational prayer with Jesus or spontaneous prayers. Just as people who grow in love change the way they converse, so too you may see your prayer develop. You can talk with Jesus as you would talk to a friend.

We have discussed feeling God's love and the gift of salvation given freely to us through Jesus. In this session, we will try to picture what the new life in God might be like.

The Father wants all people to have a new life. He wants nothing but the best for his children. Jesus said, "I came that you might have life, and have it to the full" (John 10:10). Jesus wants us to be filled with enthusiasm and the constant awareness of his love. This is possible by choosing to let Jesus take charge of our life, by letting him take the front seat of our bike. His Holy Spirit becomes more apparent in our life as we surrender more to him.

In accepting his lordship, we feel a new freedom. Every barrier between us and the Father can be removed. This opens the door for the power of the Holy Spirit to be released in us, which changes us (Romans 8:14–17). We feel a new, deeper relationship with "*Abba.*" This love relationship gives us the courage to surrender more of our abilities to God's will and purpose for our lives. We are being transformed.

In this session, I will share my testimony of how I experienced the power of the Holy Spirit. It is not the only way to do it, but it is the way it happened to me. Perhaps you will identify with some of the things I felt as I made this journey. I must say that the first time I went through this retreat many years ago, I did not think I needed it. I was going to skip the retreat, but the leader encouraged me to at least check it out for a day. That first day, the leader began talking about listening prayer and surrendering my will to God. I realized that often, when I prayed, I told Jesus what I wanted rather than listening to what he wanted to tell me. After hearing about listening to God, I decided to try it. I went into the chapel and sat in the presence of God. I sat right up in front. I kept telling Jesus that I came to listen to him that evening. It took me 45 minutes to quiet my mind. After finally getting myself quiet, I heard Jesus say, "Paul, I love you." I had known that in my head, but that night I felt it like never before. The tears flowed as I sat in his presence for a long time. I never felt that much love from him. It was overwhelming. I walked out of the chapel as a different person. After that, I wanted to surrender my will to his.

The following days, I listened for his direction. I asked him what he needed me to study to prepare for priestly ministry. I felt his direction as I offered him all my abilities. I changed some behaviors and spent a half hour every morning reading the scripture and getting to know what his voice sounded like. I no longer did things to earn his love; rather, I did them because he loved me. His love empowered me. In the following days, I read through the whole New Testament. I could not stop reading through the gospels. I came to feel Jesus' great compassion and care for people and for me. I read the apostle Paul's letters and finally understood how he could endure so much suffering for Jesus. He was a man in love with God, and he had the fire of the Holy Spirit in his heart.

At this point in my life, I had been studying to be a priest for six and a half years, but I realized that I had never asked Jesus if that was what he wanted for my life. It was terrifying to ask him if he wanted me to be his priest because I do not know what I would have done if he said no. I realized that if he did not want me to be a priest, it would be foolish to do it. I finally surrendered my vocation and listened to see if I was on the right path. I did not tell anyone about this decision to surrender and listen. After choosing to listen, many unsolicited messages came to me that confirmed my life choice. A couple of weeks following this decision, my friend brought me a birthday card for my twenty-first birthday. He said he received a message for me. He wrote it on the card. It said, "Paul, a servant of Christ Jesus, called to be an apostle and set apart to proclaim the gospel of God" (Romans 1:1). I could not believe that God would speak so clearly. Also, during the following months, many people approached me and confirmed my preparation for priesthood. Once I knew that God was calling me to ministry, I had the strength and courage to face whatever it took to carry out what Jesus called me to be. My ministry has turned out to be much larger and more anointed than I could have ever dreamed. Listening to Jesus and feeling the anointing of the Holy Spirit became a way of life.

I was hesitant to accept the gifts of the Holy Spirit (i.e., prayer in tongues, prophecy, healing, words of knowledge), but as I kept letting Jesus be in charge, I experienced each of these gifts somewhat by surprise. As I needed them, the Holy Spirit provided them. I learned to relax and let God move in me according to his will. Life got much more exciting as I did things I knew were more than I could do alone. When I saw the first healing, I knew God was taking me on a unique journey. I learned to keep listening and holding on. The journey has not stopped after fifty years.

Your journey will be different, but if you keep listening and surrendering, it will be exciting and larger than you can imagine. This week, we reflect on various aspects of a new, transformed life in Jesus. Be open to all that God has for you. Listen to God's message through the daily reflections during your quiet time. Be open to the gifts of the Holy Spirit manifesting in your life. With time, you can expect the fruits of the Spirit to "ripen" in you as well.

Questions

Are there any things you do not understand about this new life in the power of the Holy Spirit?

Are you open to listening for God's voice and receiving his love for you?

What gifts of the Holy Spirit might you need to enhance your care for other people?

Take *15 minutes of quiet time* every day this week and soak in the following scriptures and reflections.

Day 1

A transformed life filled with the gifts of the Holy Spirit is available to every person. Jesus said, "I came that you might have life and have it to the full" (John 10:10).

Day 2

God promises to cleanse our hearts with his love and create them anew, enabling us to feel his loving purpose for our lives. God said, "I will sprinkle clean water upon you to cleanse you of all your impurities, and from all your idols I will cleanse you. I will give you a new heart and place a new spirit within you. . . you shall be my people and I will be your God" (Ezekiel 36:25–28).

Day 3

Before he died, Jesus promised to send the Holy Spirit to his followers. This promise of Jesus is for everyone. He said, "If you love me and obey the commands I give you, I will ask the Father and he will give you another Paraclete (Spirit) to be with you always, a Spirit of truth, whom the world cannot accept, since it neither sees him nor recognizes him; but you can recognize him because he remains with you and will be within you. I will not leave you orphaned" (John 14:15–18).

Day 4

On Pentecost, Jesus' disciples gathered together in prayer, open to feeling his loving presence. The Holy Spirit came upon them, and from that moment on, they were changed, transformed people. We read, "When the day of Pentecost came, it found them gathered in one place. . . All were filled with the Holy Spirit. They began to express themselves in foreign tongues and make bold proclamations as the Spirit prompted them" (Acts 2:1–4).

Day 5

It was normal for people in the early church to experience the gifts of the Holy Spirit at their baptism. You can also receive these gifts as you renew your baptism with an open heart. We read, "When they heard Paul's explanation, they were baptized in the name of Jesus. As Paul laid his hands on them, the Holy Spirit came down on them and they began to speak in tongues and utter prophecies" (Acts 19:5–6).

Day 6

As the Spirit pervades your life, the Spirit will equip you with spiritual gifts. They are given to you for the benefit of the community. Paul wrote about these gifts in this way: "To each person the manifestation of the Spirit is given for the common good. To one the Spirit gives wisdom in discourse, to another the power to express knowledge. Through the Spirit one receives faith; by the same Spirit another is given the gift of healing, and still another miraculous powers. Prophecy is given to one; to another power to distinguish one spirit from another. One receives the gift of tongues, another that of interpreting the tongue. But it is one and the same Spirit who produces all these gifts, distributing them to each as he wills" (1 Corinthians 12:7–11).

Day 7

When the Holy Spirit is released in you, you will begin to experience a new kind of life. You will know and feel God in a new way. That new life will grow in you, and you will begin to see the fruits of the Spirit in your life. Paul wrote, "The fruit of the Spirit is love, joy, peace, patient endurance, kindness, generosity, faith, mildness, and chastity" (Galatians 5:22–23).

Other scriptures you might wish to read this week are Luke 15, John 4, and Acts 2.

SESSION FOUR—*RECEIVING GOD'S LIFE*

(Below is a summary of the teaching for session four.
Quiet yourself and receive it into your heart.)

We talked about feeling God's love, making a choice to listen to him, and discovering what this new life looks like. Now, we ask the Father for strength to turn away from things that block our relationship with him. We do a positive repentance. This is not just reflecting on how we have hampered God from being central in our lives but seeking positive things we can do to make him more central in our thoughts and behavior. We ask the Spirit to help us examine and change our ways.

Three words on which we might reflect are honesty, humility, and surrender.

It is easy to fall into a pattern of self-deception and to become blinded to faults we are used to living with. To grow deeper in a relationship with Jesus, we must be very honest with ourselves. God is merciful to those who admit their mistakes and ask for forgiveness. Feeling God's love for us empowers us to be honest with ourselves and name where we are out of line with Jesus' teaching. Then, out of love for God, we will desire to change and become more like Jesus. It is helpful to do a serious moral inventory. We may go to a pastor or spiritual director to share that inventory and receive prayer for God's forgiveness. Many people find that to be a time of great relief and experience of God's generous mercy.

We must be humble enough to admit that we need God's help to achieve the fullness of life. God's deep love can heal our wounds if we are humble enough to ask him. Our woundedness is often the core reason we act out of line with Jesus' teachings. With God's help, we can heal those wounds. It is important that we take time to forgive others. Unforgiveness is the greatest block to healing and inner peace.

Finally, then, we surrender completely to God's will. We ask God to be the center of each day and listen for his love and guidance. We let go of our need to control and let him guide the way.

Through reading the scriptures, we get used to knowing what his voice sounds like.

Perhaps the most beautiful story in the gospel of receiving God's gift of new life and inner healing is the story of Jesus ministering to the woman at the well (John 4:7–19, 25–30, 39–42). You might wish to read the story. Jesus invites the woman to a deeper love relationship for which she has been thirsting a long time. She was looking to all kinds of men, but none could fill her spiritual needs. She was looking for something more in life. As the conversation begins, she is defensive, telling Jesus he is not supposed to talk with her. Perhaps she was afraid or was feeling unworthy or ashamed. We may feel the same at times. Jesus keeps gently persisting that he has a special love relationship for her, a living water that will quench her deepest thirst. He offers you the same gift.

When she finally opens herself a little to his love, he tells her she needs to be honest with him and call her husband. Even though she first resists, Jesus gently and persistently keeps on loving her into freedom. She comes to realize that he is not just another man. Now, the woman feels Jesus' pure love and care and is willing to change her ways. She puts down her vessel for carrying water because now she becomes the vessel that carries living water to the many thirsty people in her village. She had avoided these people earlier that day, but her conversation with Jesus healed her heart and gave her the courage to go to them with a message they all needed to hear. Her honesty, humility, and surrender to Jesus' way can be a model for us as we prepare to receive God's gift of new life. Jesus wants to fill our vessels with living water, with unconditional love.

Jesus invites us to examine our lives and repent, if necessary, for all that is not in right relationship with him. He promises his deep love to heal the memories of when we have been wounded so that we can live in the fullness of life and with a spirituality of openness to his love and will. We will then have living water to share with the people we love.

We may experience obstacles such as pride, doubts that such surrender is necessary, feelings of unworthiness, or fear of what others will think. These obstacles to a fulfilling life in the Spirit can only stop us if we allow them to. Jesus' love is greater and more powerful than all of these. We are invited to let go and drink in all the love Jesus has for us. Nothing inside of us or outside of us can stop us from accepting this gift.

Questions

What do you expect or want to happen as you surrender to Jesus and pray for his Spirit, his love, to fill you?

What things do you feel might be blocking you from receiving the new, transformed life in God's Spirit?

Are you ready to make a moral inventory and perhaps share it with one other person?

In the next section, we would usually pray with each other in the group for a full release of the Holy Spirit in each person's life. I invite you to prepare for a renewal of your Baptismal Vows and a readiness to pray a Prayer of Commitment to God. If you do not have anyone making this retreat with you, you can pray by yourself, aware that I pray daily for people who are seeking this new life in God's Spirit.

Take 15 minutes of quiet time every day this week and soak in the following scriptures and reflections.

Day 1

God has always loved you and wants you to feel cherished by him. You can put your name in this message that God spoke through the prophet Hosea. "When Israel was a child, I loved him, I called my son. The more I called them, the further they went from me. Yet it was I who taught them to walk, who took them in my arms; I drew them with human cords, with bands of love; I fostered them like one who raises an infant to his creeks, yet though I stooped to feed my child, they did not know that I was their healer" (Hosea 11:1–4).

Day 2

God has a new life for us because he loves us. It is a gift. We cannot earn it. We read, "When the kindness and love of God our Savior appeared, he saved us, not because of any righteous deeds we had done, but because of his mercy. He saved us through the baptism of new birth and renewal by the Holy Spirit, lavished on us through Jesus our Savior (Titus 3:4–6).

Day 3

To receive the fullness of God's life, we must turn away from everything incompatible with the life God is offering and accept the promises God is making. When we turn to Jesus in repentance and faith, he can give this new life to us. Jesus said, "This is the time of fulfillment. The reign of God is at hand. Reform your lives and believe in the gospel" (Mark 1:15).

Day 4

This new life with Jesus is for everyone who will turn to him. The gift of the Holy Spirit is for you. We read, "You must reform and be baptized, each one of you, in the name of Jesus Christ, that your sins may be forgiven; then you will receive the gift of the Holy Spirit. It was to you and your children that the promise was made, and to all those still far off whom the Lord our God calls" (Acts 2:38–39).

Day 5

Jesus desires to give you a new, transformed way of life that is more peaceful, happier, and better than the old. We must actively seek to put away our old self to experience more of this new freedom in Jesus. Paul wrote, "You must lay aside your former way of life and the old self which deteriorates through illusion and desire, and acquire a fresh, spiritual way of thinking. You must put on the new person created in God's image, whose justice and holiness are born of truth" (Ephesians 4:22–23).

Day 6

Jesus wants his Spirit to flow freely through every area of your being. Let his life, his love, quench your deepest thirst. Jesus said, "Whoever drinks the water I give will never be thirsty; no, the water I give shall become a fountain within him, leaping up to provide eternal life" (John 4:14).

Day 7

Jesus promised that the Father would give the Holy Spirit to those who ask. He said, "So I say to you, 'Ask and you shall receive; seek and you shall find; knock and it shall be opened to you.' . . . What father among you will give his son a snake if he asks for a fish, or hand him a scorpion if he asks for an egg? If you, with all your sins, know how to give your children good things, how much more will the heavenly Father give the Holy Spirit to those who ask him" (Luke 11:9–11).

Other scriptures you might wish to read this week are Luke 24, John 16, and Romans 8.

SESSION FIVE—*RELEASING GOD'S SPIRIT*

(Below is a summary of how this session flows.)

You begin this session by renewing your baptismal promises, since you will be praying for the release of the power of your baptism.

Then, quiet yourself and pray through the Prayer for Inner Healing.

Next, pray the Prayer of Commitment to God.

After that, if you have a group, you can take time to pray with each other for a full release of God's Spirit with all the gifts of the Spirit. If you are alone, sit in your place of prayer and take a long, quiet time to receive what God wants to pour out on you.

Baptismal Vows

Do you renounce sin so as to live in the freedom of God's children?
I do.
Do you renounce all evil powers and refuse to be mastered by sin?
I do.
Do you renounce Satan, father of sin and prince of darkness?
I do.
Do you turn to Jesus Christ and accept him as your Lord and Savior?
I do.
Do you put your whole trust in his grace and love?
I do.
Do you promise to follow and obey Jesus as your Lord?
I do.

Prayer for Inner Healing

Jesus, thank you for being here, for the privilege of feeling your strength and your presence. You can walk back through my life, back to the very moment I was conceived. Help me, Jesus, even then. Cleanse my bloodlines and free me of all those things that may have caused me difficulty at the moment of conception. When I was formed within my mother's womb, you were there; free me and heal me of any binds upon my spirit that may have entered me through my mother or the circumstances of my parents' lives even as I was being formed. For this, I give you thanks.

I praise you, Jesus, that you are healing me also of the trauma of being born. I pray, Jesus, that you would heal me of the pain of birth and all I went through being born. Thank you for being there to receive me into your arms as I came into this world. Consecrate me in that moment to the service of your Father. I thank you, Jesus, for this has been done.

Lord Jesus, I praise you that in those early months of infancy, you were there with me when I needed you. There were times I needed my mother to hold me close, to rock me, and tell me the little stories that only a mother can. For the times this did not happen, Jesus, do this for me now in the very depths of my being. Let me feel such an overwhelming sense of maternal, comforting, nourishing love that nothing will ever separate me from that love again. I thank you and praise you, Jesus, because I know it is being done.

For the times I did not get the father's love that I needed, Father God, fill in that part of my being now with your strong fatherly love that comes only from a father. Even if I am not aware of having needed to have strong arms around me and "daddy" to love me and give me security and strength, do that for me now. Thank you for your treasured love.

I have come to understand and accept it, but a part of me never really felt complete, never really felt wanted. I ask you today for a healing of that. Let me know today that I am your child, and important person in your family, a unique individual that you love in a very special way.

Heal me, Jesus, of the hurts that came because of the relationships in my family, the brother or sister that did not quite understand me or were not able to show me kindness. Part of me never felt loved because of it. Heal those places in me and guide me to a healthy community where I can be loved into wholeness.

I pray, Jesus, for a healing of those years I spent in the classroom. Take from me any pain or suffering that was inflicted upon me at that time. I withdrew within myself then, Jesus. I began to be afraid to speak out in groups because I had been ridiculed, chastised, or criticized in classroom situations. I stopped speaking up because it was too painful. Jesus, I ask that the door within my heart be opened. With the strength of your Spirit, help me relate in groups more openly and freely than I have ever been able to. As this healing takes place, I will have the confidence and courage to do what you call me to do in every situation. I thank you, Jesus, because I believe this is being healed now.

Jesus, as I went into adolescence, I began to experience things that frightened me, embarrassed me, and caused me pain. I have never quite gotten over some of my experiences in learning about myself and what it means to be a man/woman. I pray, Jesus, for healing upon all those experiences that I had as a teenager, for the things I did, and for the things that were done to me which have never quite been healed. Enter my heart and heal me now of all the experiences that have caused me suffering, embarrassment, or shame. I am not asking you to erase these things from my mind but to transform them so that I can remember them no longer with shame but with thanksgiving. Thank you, Jesus, that this is being done.

Jesus, as I emerged from that period in my life and began to grow into the vocation into which you called me, I had difficulties. I ask you to heal me of the injuries that I received in the early years of adulthood and the vocation that I am in. Free me to do what you ask of me without the hinderance of past wounds.

(For those who are married.) Jesus, I pray for healing of the pains that words and actions may have caused in my marriage. Let my marriage begin again to be what you have called it to be. Let all the old hurts and sorrows be put into your hands so that from this moment on, this marriage can be cleansed and begun anew, as free and as healed as it can be. Thank you, Jesus, that through your healing love we can become the kind of husband and wife you have asked us to be.

Help me, Jesus, to feel such warmth and strength of love pouring into me that I will never again doubt the path I'm traveling is the one on which you have called me to be. Give me courage and confidence in the work that you have called me to do. Carry me forward with a newness of purpose and goals. Let me be a living witness for you. Thank you, Jesus, for I know this is being done.

As the anointing of your love flows over me, I praise you, Jesus. There is no power in heaven or earth that can stop it. I praise you, Jesus, because I know that the more I give to you, thanking you and praising you for it, the more you will give me the strength of your presence, the power of your Spirit, the love from your divine heart. I praise you, Jesus, for this healing and give you the glory. Thank you. Amen.

(You might take some quiet time and let Jesus do his healing work in you, emptying your heart of things that are not of God. Let Jesus refill it with his love.)

When you are ready, I invite you to pray the following prayer.

Prayer of Commitment to God.

Father, I thank you for giving me the gift of life and for revealing Jesus to me as my Lord. I have been seeking to make Jesus the Lord of every part of my mind, my heart, and my will. In your gentle love, you have brought me to this moment.

At this moment, I declare my deep desire to experience a fuller release of your Holy Spirit in my life. Fill me with new life. Restore me to baptismal innocence and fervor. Make me strong in resisting sin and eager to proclaim the Good News of your mercy and faithful love.

I now renew any vows that I have made in light of your lordship over my life. Jesus, let your Spirit empower me the way that Spirit empowered your first disciples at Pentecost. From now on, I want you to be the Lord of my life. Thank you, Father, Son, and Holy Spirit. I praise and adore you present in me.

(If you have a group, you can now gently and quietly lay hands on each other and pray for a full release of the Holy Spirit with all the gifts of the Holy Spirit. If you are alone, you can quietly soak in the Spirit flowing over you. Continue praising God.)

Take 15 *minutes of quiet time* every day this week and soak in the following scriptures and reflections.

Day 1

Through your commitment and prayer, God can work more freely in you. Rejoice in God's presence and thank him for the gift of new life. Paul wrote, "Rejoice in the Lord always. I say it again, rejoice. Everyone should see how unselfish you are. The Lord is near. Dismiss all anxiety from your minds. Present your needs to God in every form of prayer and petition full of gratitude. Then God's own peace, which is beyond understanding, will stand guard over your hearts and minds, in Christ Jesus" (Philippians 4:4–7).

Day 2

Jesus promised, "The Holy Spirit whom the Father will send in my name, will instruct you in everything and remind you of all that I told you. Peace is my farewell to you; my peace is my gift to you; I do not give it to you as the world gives peace" (John 14:26–27).

Day 3

When you live in the Spirit, the Spirit prays in you. Let the Spirit pray in you often during the day, sometimes in English and sometimes in the new tongue you may have been given. Paul wrote, "At every opportunity pray in the Spirit, using prayers and petitions of every sort" (Ephesians 6:18).

Day 4

Learn to set your mind and heart on God and the things of the Spirit. Take time to ponder the words of life that Jesus speaks to you through scripture or your time of inner stillness. You will find new peace and serenity as Jesus' message transforms your mind and heart. We read, "The tendency of the flesh is toward death but that of the Spirit toward life and peace" (Romans 8:6).

Day 5

Jesus has blessed you with spiritual gifts to serve him effectively. These gifts are a way of expressing your love for God and his people. Showing your love for God and others is central to the new life. Paul says, "Seek eagerly after love. Set your hearts on spiritual gifts" (1 Corinthians 14:1).

Day 6

To deepen our relationship with God, we must pray. Jesus prayed often. Although Jesus was the Son of God, he still had to spend time with *Abba*. We must talk to God often if we wish to stay alive spiritually. We read, "Jesus' reputation spread more and more, and great crowds gathered to hear him and to be cured of their maladies. He often retired to deserted places and prayed" (Luke 5:15–16).

Day 7

Through Jesus, we receive the power to handle challenging situations. Paul wrote, "This treasure we possess in earthen vessels, to make it clear that its surpassing power comes from God and not from us. We are afflicted in every way possible, but we are not crushed; full of doubts, we never despair. We are persecuted but never abandoned; we are struck down but never destroyed.

Continually we carry in our bodies the dying of Jesus, so that in our bodies the life of Jesus may also be revealed" (2 Corinthians 4:7–10).

Other scriptures you might wish to read this week are John 15, Philippians 2, and Galatians 5.

SESSION SIX—*GROWTH AND TRANSFORMATION*

(Below is a summary of the teaching for session six. Quiet yourself and receive it into your heart.)

Last week, you prayed for the full release of the Holy Spirit in you. You may feel a new joy and peace and desire to praise God in a new way. Whatever you feel, know that the power of the Holy Spirit has been released in you, and it will grow as you nurture it. Jesus said, "I am the vine and you are the branches. The one who lives in me and I am in him will produce abundantly, for apart from me you can do nothing. . . If you live in me, and my words stay part of you, you may ask what you will and it will be done for you. My Father has been glorified in your bearing much fruit and becoming my disciples" (John 15:5–8).

Jesus gave us the image of the vine and the branches to let us know that we need to draw energy from him continually. This happens by staying connected to him. This week, we look at four main ways of receiving God's love to continue to live a transformed life. We want to stay vibrant with his love.

The first way to grow in a love relationship with Jesus is through daily personal prayer. Dedicate at least 15 minutes every day to listen to Jesus as you did during the retreat. Take time to praise Jesus, read his word, and listen for his gentle words of love. No matter how busy we are, this is the most important time to connect with him and receive direction for the day.

The second important part of spiritual growth is studying and getting to know Jesus in scripture, in the traditions of the church, and through spiritual writers. We want to renew not only our hearts but also our minds. We study to let Jesus' worldview overcome the worldview of the culture. We begin to see events as Jesus sees them, which gives us hope and security. We will look at this more deeply in the next chapter.

The third means of receiving life from Jesus is through community. This is essential to life in the Spirit. Christianity has always been a communal religion. We need to be with people who will remind us of God's love. Try to connect with people who will help you stay focused on Jesus and who are also seeking to be transformed. This may be through a Prayer Group, a Bible Study group, a particular church group, or family members. When I led people through this retreat, they often wanted to stay together and continue to meet. We would gather weekly, sing praise songs to God, share scripture readings which spoke to us that week, and sometimes have someone share a brief spiritual teaching. We would end with more songs. Be ready for whatever opportunity Jesus opens for you.

You might try to find a healing community where you can receive the healing love of Jesus and give it to others. The Order of St. Luke is an organization of numerous healing communities around the country. Their website can be found at the end of this book in the "Further Reading." If you are in a sacramental church, use the sacraments to enrich your walk with Jesus. Sunday Eucharist or Holy Communion is a profound way to renew your commitment to Jesus as he commits his body and blood for you.

The fourth way to grow closer to God is through serving others. As you serve others by giving the gift of God's love, you share what you have discovered, and it becomes more solidified in you. Right after I went through this retreat, the leader asked me to help with the next one he was leading. That experience helped me internalize these teachings. God may open other avenues for you to serve. Even if they challenge you a little, that is when you can feel the help of the Holy Spirit. This deep awareness of God's love for you empowers you to serve, build up others, and share this great gift. You live out God's destiny for you by first listening to his purpose for you and then using his power to accomplish it.

I encourage you to avoid discouragement. Trust God's promises that we read through this retreat. Read them again and again. Many people do not notice a huge change right away in their lives, but if they keep taking in God's love every day, after a couple of months, they see how they have become more like Jesus. Even if you are not feeling immediate changes, stay faithful to the process, and the gifts and fruits of the Spirit will develop in your life. Jesus is the vine, and his energy keeps flowing to those of us who are connected. There is always more energy to come.

Questions

What will you do differently than what you have done to this point in your life to nurture your new life? Maybe one of the four ways mentioned? Without making some changes, people usually go back to their old ways.

What is the most powerful thing you have learned or felt through this retreat?

Are you willing to read more about becoming a transformed person? Are you willing to be gently bold in talking with others about God's deep love for them?

Take *15 minutes of quiet time* every day this week and soak in the following scriptures and reflections.

Day 1

Real life comes from Jesus. Remain connected to him. Jesus said, "I am the vine and you are the branches. The one who lives in me and I in him will produce abundantly, for apart from me you can do nothing" (John 15:5).

Day 2

There is nothing as precious as knowing Jesus and belonging to him. Not only do your lives become more fruitful, but you have a very deep, pervasive joy and serenity. That is a treasure. Paul wrote, "I have come to rate all as loss in light of the surpassing knowledge of my Lord Jesus Christ. For his sake I have forfeited everything; I have accounted all as rubbish so that Christ may be my wealth and I may be in him" (Philippians 3:8–9).

Day 3

Trials may come as you deepen your commitment to Jesus. Others may misunderstand you and try to make you give up your journey. You may have doubts, fears, and confusion at times, but these can be means of growth if you walk through them in faith. The apostle James wrote, "Count it pure joy when you are involved in every sort of trial. Realize that when your faith is tested, this makes for endurance. Let endurance come to its perfection so that you may be fully mature and lacking in nothing" (James 1:2–4).

Day 4

Jesus is with you. He loves you and will always remain close to you, no matter what challenges you have to face. Paul wrote, "God will not let you be tested beyond your strength. Along with any test, he will give you a way out of it so that you may be able to endure it" (1 Corinthians 10:13).

Day 5

If you are faithful to Jesus and love him, everything will work out for the good. There is nothing that can separate you from God's love. We read, "We know that God makes all things work together for the good of those who have been called according to his decree. . . If God is for us, who can be against us?" (Romans 8:28–31)

Day 6

If you feel Jesus' love for you, you can feel his love for others, especially those in your community. We can feel closely connected to other people who are seeking to be transformed. Paul wrote, "Just as each of us has one body with many members, and not all the members have the same function, so too we, though many, are one body in Christ and individually members one of another" (Romans 12:4–5).

Day 7

Jesus is working in you to give you a better life and make you whole. This transformation may take time. After many years of ministry, Paul wrote, "It is not that I have reached it yet, or have already finished my course; but I am racing to grasp the prize if possible, since I have been grasped by Jesus Christ. I do not think of myself as having reached the finish line. I give no thought to what lies behind, but push on to what is ahead" (Philippians 3:12–13).

Other scriptures you might wish to read this week are John 17, Philippians 3, Luke 10.

CONCLUDING SUMMARY

You have been given a very valuable gift—life in God's Spirit. God gave you the gift of his life because he loves you, and you took time to seek and receive him. Keep your eyes on him as you journey on. No one can take you away from him. Jesus says to you, "Do not let your hearts be troubled. Have faith in God and faith in me" (John 14:1).

Have no fear, for Jesus is with you. He will care for you with gentleness and love. With Jesus' Spirit in you, nothing can overcome you.

All your problems have not been solved. You are not yet perfect, but you have "the way, the truth, and the life" in you. You have the power of the Holy Spirit in you.

Paul wrote, "If God is for us, who can be against us? . . . For I am certain that neither death nor life, neither angels, nor principalities, neither the present nor the future, nor powers, neither height nor depth nor any other creature, will be able to separate us from the love of God that comes to us in Christ Jesus, our Lord" (Romans 8:31–39).

You may wish to revisit this retreat more often to soak in the power and energy of these scriptures. Every time I lead this retreat and walk this journey, I hear something more.

CHAPTER 3

A Time to Listen and Heal

Now that we have made this retreat and had time to soak in God's love for us, we can move on to various areas that may need healing and further exploring. God's love is what heals. It is the same love that created us. It recreates us when we take time to feel it and absorb it into our being. As we begin being transformed, we notice a new view of life, which opens us to the healing power of God. We can discover how feeling God's love empowers inner healing of past hurts and wounded memories that we may have carried through life. This love was present to us at conception and has been there all along. Now, we can go back and experience God's perfect love in our life story and receive it to heal our memories. We began doing that through the Prayer for Inner Healing, which we prayed during session five. We can do that often, gradually inviting God's love to cleanse and heal us completely.

In this chapter, we will take time to discover ways to hear God's voice and feel the security it gives to our lives. My spiritual journey has taught me that real peace is only found by listening to the Master's voice. I would rather "do it my way," but experience has shown the fruits of "doing it his way." In the retreat, I described surrendering to Jesus' direction for my life. It was like letting him on the front seat of a two-seater bike. Giving him control seemed very scary, but I came to realize that he knows much better where my life needs to be going to find fulfillment. Once I let go, I felt a deep peace. Daily listening and surrendering are my greatest sources of inner peace.

The words of scripture that have encouraged me on my journey are found in Mark's gospel. We read, "Rising early the next morning, Jesus went off to a lonely place in the desert; there he was absorbed in prayer" (Mark 1:35). Jesus needed to renew himself in the affirming love of the Father to face the challenges of his mission. Bathing himself in that love empowered him to respond with such compassion to the sick and meet his attackers with inner strength and courage. It also guided his travels to where the Father desired. When we listen and submit to his voice, we not only get a sense of direction and peace but also get flooded with God's love to carry out whatever he asks of us. When we are in his will, we can handle challenges beyond our abilities. That is when we experience the gifts of the Holy Spirit.

Not long after I completely surrendered my life to Jesus, I witnessed my first healing. I discovered the power of God's love flowing through me and the joy of listening to Jesus' direction. A small group of us felt called to go into the hospital hallways and sing worship songs. That is something I would never have done on my own. When we finished, a nurse came out of a room and told us that the man in the room asked us to pray for him. We entered the room, and there was a man lying on the bed in a full-body cast. Only his face was visible. He told us that he had been in a skiing accident which seriously injured his neck. He said that he had spent the last nine weeks in this body cast. He asked, "Would you pray with me for healing? Tomorrow they will cut off the cast, and they said I would have much pain." I had never prayed with someone like that before, but I felt God was directing it. We put our hands on his cast and asked God's love to heal him. Then, we went back to the seminary where we lived. The next morning, he called me up all excited. He asked, "What did you do to me yesterday?" He said that when the doctor cut off the cast, he moved his head from side to side and had no pain. This was a great surprise to the doctor. Then, when they took him for X-rays, they repeated them four times because they could not believe the results. His neck, where he had been injured, now looked perfect. He kept asking, "What did you do to me?" I said, "I don't know, but I am going to find out." That began my journey to discover more about the healing ministry of Jesus. I studied every scripture and read all I could to discover the essence of Jesus' healing ministry. I found that he was receiving the Father's love continually and then sharing it abundantly with those he met. I realized that being in the Master's will and receiving his love opens the door for the Holy Spirit to flow through us. Stepping out to do what God asks can be scary, but it offers deep joy and peace. We may find ourselves doing things we never did before or things that we thought were impossible.

The inner decision to listen for God's voice is the first step toward a richer life filled with deep peace and serenity. It means that we are open to acting on what we hear, doing what God asks. It is easier to do after we experience God's love for us. If we know God's direction is coming out of love, then it is not difficult to obey, even if we cannot see God's overall plan for our life.

To listen means that we need to quiet ourselves. In a world filled with noise, this can be a challenge. It takes some intentional effort, but the fruits of hearing God's voice are worth it. Like Jesus, we need to "go off alone" to be in the Divine presence. During the retreat, I encouraged you to take at least 15 minutes of quiet time every day. It is a way to start. If we desire it, there is a quiet spot for each of us. During one of these six-week retreats, a man decided to use his lunch break to spend time with Jesus. He closed his office door, pulled his "Refection" booklet out of the middle drawer of his desk, and took time to be quiet and listen. He said it made the rest of the day go so much easier.

One young couple with two little boys explained to them that they had to go and play at this certain time because Mom and Dad wanted to be quiet with Jesus. After a couple of days, the parents did not see the children in their room. They started looking around the house, and eventually, they opened a lower cabinet door and found the two boys in there. They asked, "What are you doing in here?" The boys said, "We are taking our quiet time with Jesus."

Whatever space we find and whatever time of the day works best, taking quiet time with Jesus is essential to staying closely connected to him and experiencing the security of hearing his voice. There is not one way for all. Our quiet time will vary depending on our personality type and life situation. Some people have a prayer chair and a space with a candle or a picture of Jesus. Some find a bench in the woods to be their spot to hear and feel Jesus. Some stop in a church on their way to or from work. The crucial thing is that we decide to do it.

I have journeyed with many people who have decided to quiet themselves and listen. Often, they say that their mind wanders off. I struggled with that, also. One help is to have a short scripture reading, as we did in the retreat, to keep us focused. Some people use a phrase like, "Jesus, Son of God, have mercy on me." Even with this help our mind can wander. It is normal. When I find my mind thinking of something else, I bring that into my conversation with Jesus. For example, my head will go off thinking about what I will say in the sermon for the weekend. When I notice that, I talk with Jesus about what he wants me to speak about in my sermon and ask him to anoint my words. Then, I go back to praising him. If I start thinking of a person I have to meet that day, I talk with Jesus about that person and ask him to anoint our meeting. The important thing is that we do not feel ashamed about our mind wandering. Jesus understands and welcomes us to come back to our conversation with him.

I have worked with many people who seek to quiet themselves and hear God's voice. Some would say, "I am afraid to be still because then feelings of sadness or anger come up." Some mention that they feel unworthy to take time with God. Some feel a block in trying to hear God's voice amid so many inner voices. It is exactly these things that set the stage for the rich benefits of listening prayer.

In the quiet, we find out what unresolved feelings we might be carrying, and then we are in a position to surrender them to God's love and experience inner healing. I often ask people, "What happens when you seek quiet time with God? If they get sad, we begin looking for the root of the unresolved grief that they are carrying. Once they name the core of the grief, we can go back and see Jesus with them in that time of loss and release the pain into his hands. Then, we invite his love to fill the void left by the loss. This inner healing brings a sense of relief and a new joy.

At times, people say they get angry when they are quiet. When we seek the root, we often find a deep hurt at the core of the anger. We take time to see Jesus back in that time when the hurt occurred and then ask his love to heal it. Because Jesus was there, the person can feel his presence and release the hurt. We sometimes discover that the hurt has become resentment, and they have not forgiven the person who hurt them. We talk about the fact that not forgiving is only holding themselves in prison and is not hurting the other person. Gradually, we can get to the point of praying a blessing for the person who hurt them. Choosing to forgive releases the resentment and opens the person to inner healing.

Some people live with a high level of fear or anxiety. They stay busy and always on the go, so they do not feel the fear. I help them search for the root of their fear, the time it started, and then invite Jesus into that moment. Once they feel Jesus' love in that root event, the fear begins to subside. This inner healing works because Jesus was there, loving them in that moment. Feeling the security of God's love brings a deep inner peace. It is helpful to have someone who believes in healing prayer to pray with us as we release any unresolved feelings that surface when we quiet ourselves.

Many people carry a strong "shame voice" within. They feel unworthy to talk with God. I listen to their "shame voice" and help them identify whose voice it is. Often it is a parent's voice who may have called them stupid or just never gave them positive compliments. We begin with forgiving the person who shamed them. Then, we listen to the voice of Jesus in the gospels, and they realize Jesus does not shame anyone. He is a no-shaming presence where they can find affirmation and a sense of being valued. This allows them to dispel the "shame voice" from their mind and receive the affirming voice of Jesus. They discover their true dignity as sons/

daughters of the Father. If they become members of a non-shaming community, they become even more sure of their true identity.

Quieting ourselves has the great benefit of making us aware of what feelings we may be repressing. These repressed feelings wreak havoc on our bodies, tearing at our organs and diminishing our immune system. Discovering what feelings we are repressing puts us in a position for inner healing, which often brings about physical healing. In his book, *Breaking Emotional Barriers to Healing*, Craig Miller offers many compelling stories of how physical healing often happens when we take time for inner healing. He describes many physical healings occurring when he helped people experience inner healing. His method of taking Jesus and another safe person back to the origin of the memory and creating a safe environment to release the repressed emotion is a very effective way of experiencing healing of that memory. If unresolved emotions come up, we may need to find someone who can help us release them. Our bodies are not made to carry unresolved feelings or wounded memories. Taking quiet time and feeling God's love for us opens the way for us to let go of destructive repressed feelings we may have carried for a long time. It allows us to live a peaceful and serene life. Studies show that 92% of physical disease has an emotional root. Releasing these repressed emotions improves and extends our life. Stepping through the fear of quieting ourselves and honestly looking within, surrounded by God's love, opens the door to releasing these unhealthy sources of stress and discovering God's healing power.

Inner quieting can have other benefits, also. I remember one woman who came to the retreat to experience God's love. She quieted herself for the first weeks but soon noticed something she had to deal with. She came to me and said, "If I am going to grow closer to God, I need to confess something of my past." She confessed her sin, and I prayed for Jesus' forgiveness to flow over her and release her guilt. She then could continue her journey to a transformed life. The guilt she carried for years and the daily stress that it caused was gone. She finished the retreat and eventually became a leader in the community.

I notice that when I quiet myself every day and surrender to God's will, I do not have a need to retaliate when someone takes their anger out on me. It keeps me grounded in Jesus' peace. I recall the day a young couple came into my office to prepare for the baptism of their four little daughters. I talked to the girls about the love they could feel from God when I baptized them and explained to the parents their role in helping their children learn about Jesus. All the while we talked, the father kept making quite nasty remarks about me and what I was saying. Instead of reacting to his words, I felt his pain. I finally said, "Your dad must have been hard on you." Immediately, he began to cry. He shared how awful his childhood was and the pain his dad had caused. He was taking his anger out on me as a father figure. My response gave him the space to release years of repressed pain and sadness. I prayed that he would feel *Abba* loving him at that moment. He felt a true Father's love for the first time, and it healed his memories. He became more excited about the baptisms and what his daughters could feel. After the baptisms, he and his wife brought their children to church every Sunday, and they all sat in the front pew. He was so happy to feel loved and accepted. I thanked God for the words and gestures to respond to his initial anger. Hearing Jesus' voice every day is a powerful tool for ministry.

Taking quiet time with Jesus has also helped me take responsibility for what I let into my mind. I can make choices about what I allow to fill my mind, what I read, what I watch on TV, and look at on the computer or phone. With all the noise and words available around us, we must intentionally decide to quiet ourselves and listen to the words of Jesus in the scripture. We do not have to listen to all the news every day or have our phone on all the time. Taking a quiet walk with Jesus is much more refreshing and life-giving. We read that Jesus "often retired to deserted places and prayed." Keeping our minds empty of unnecessary material leaves room for Jesus to fill them with messages of love and affirmation. This allows us to live the transformed life, what Jesus called the fullness of life (John 10:10).

I also find it helpful to make two piles in my mind. On one pile are things that I can do nothing about, such as any world situations, national happenings, and other things out of my control. On the second pile are things that I can help change or effect a positive difference. If I let go of listening to or ruminating about things that I cannot change, I use up energy that I could use to improve situations that I can change. As I try to live a transformed life, I focus my gifts and abilities on people and situations I can help. It also helps me empty my mind of unnecessary clutter and receive messages from God. These messages direct my day, making for a peaceful and meaningful life.

Prayer for Inner Quiet

Jesus, I want to be quiet inside and hear your words for me. I know that your voice can give true peace to my heart. Give me the strength and desire to quiet myself each day so that your voice will be the empowering guide for my life. Fill me with the courage to trust and obey the messages you give to me. Let me feel, through your words, the deep love you have for me so that I may know the real peace and joy you have promised. Thank you, Jesus, for continually speaking words of love to me, even when I block them out with noise. Be patient with me as I slowly create quiet spaces in my life for you. You are indeed good to me, and I love you. Amen.

Questions

What changes would you make to carve out 15 minutes a day of quiet time with Jesus? Are you willing to try?

What feelings or issues would surface if you took this quiet time? Do you have someone with whom you could talk about these feelings and perhaps receive healing prayer?

Have you ever experienced the peace of taking quiet time with Jesus? Share.

Chapter 4

Looking at Our Bedrock Scriptures

We have seen what our decision to listen to Jesus can do to our heart. It fills us with a deep peace and serenity. It offers us an opportunity to release unresolved feelings and experience inner healing. In this chapter, we will look at how listening to Jesus can bring renewal to our mind. Hearing Jesus' voice gives us a divine worldview. We read, "Do not conform yourselves to this age but be transformed by the renewal of your mind, so that you may judge what is God's will, what is good, pleasing and perfect" (Romans 12:2). This renewal of our heart and mind allows us to know God more deeply and live in the power of the Holy Spirit. We let *Abba* direct our thoughts and actions, being conformed to his will and empowered by his love.

You may know many of these things if you have been part of a Christian community, but there are always new treasures to discover about Jesus' words and actions. We will examine closely what Jesus said. Jesus' teachings were quite different from those of his culture, and they are quite different than the messages of our present age. To discover his unique teachings, we need to examine the New Testament, particularly the Gospel of Mark and the letters of Paul. These are the earliest writings in the New Testament. We could call them the bedrock scriptures because they give us the most accurate picture of Jesus' heart and mind. They also show us a unique community of people who did not conform to the present age but were transformed by their relationship with Jesus.

I want to take a moment to point out that people sometimes think the Bible is a book like other books. However, the Bible is a library filled with 66 books written over about a 1,000-year period. They are a variety of genres. When we go into a library, we decide what type of book we want to read.

When we walk into the Bible, we notice that some books are more historical, some are poetry, some are stories, some are apocalyptic writings, and some give us the actual story of Jesus' life. The first 39 books tell us about God's movement in the world before Jesus came, and the last 27 tell us about Jesus and the people who followed him after his death and resurrection. The four gospels are the only books that reveal the life of Jesus. All of the books in the Bible are inspired by the Holy Spirit and can help us understand God. The thread that binds them together is that they all talk about the movement of God in history. As we saw earlier, Jesus updated some of the teachings in the books written before he came to earth. We can glean some truths from each book understood in its own time and genre. To get to know Jesus, we look primarily at the four gospels.

In this chapter, I will focus on the gospel of Mark because it is the oldest of the four gospels and gives us the best picture of the mind of Jesus and the rhythm of his heartbeat. Scripture scholars believe that the Gospel of Mark was the first gospel written. It may have been written as early as AD 40 and not later than AD 62. The apostle Paul wrote his letters between AD 49 and AD 62. Since Jesus died and rose around AD 33, these scriptures were written only 10 to 30 years after that. Many people who witnessed the resurrected presence of Jesus were still alive at that time. They were a living testimony of the truth of these writings. No other writings have this verifying testimony. This means that these writings are very reliable in giving us an accurate account of the message and actions of Jesus. In his book, *Love Your God with All Your Mind*, J. P. Moreland offers an excellent description of the reliability of the gospels and Paul's letters. They are the best source for discovering the mind and heart of Jesus. He also points out that the oral tradition that kept these stories alive until they were written down was very accurate during that time period. The storytellers needed to convey the stories exactly as they received them.

Paul's letters are some of the earliest writings after Jesus' death and resurrection, and they give us first-hand testimony of the fact that Jesus rose from the dead and was visible to many people. Paul wrote in his letter to the Corinthians around AD 57, "I handed on to you first of all what I myself received, that Jesus Christ died for our sins in accordance with the scriptures; that he was buried and, in accordance with the scriptures, rose on the third day; that he was seen by Peter, then by the twelve apostles. After that, he was seen by five hundred brothers at once, most of whom are still alive, although some have fallen asleep. Next, he was seen by James; then by all the apostles. Last of all, he was seen by me, as one born out of the normal course" (1 Corinthians 15:3–8). Paul could not have written those things if they were not true since so many people who witnessed these events were still alive.

Many of us may have believed in Jesus' resurrection for a long time, but some do not believe that he rose from the dead. They say that he was just a good teacher of his day but that he was not divine. He was a good teacher, indeed, but he was much more. He was the Son of God and the only religious leader who rose from the dead. Moreland describes in his book the compelling evidence of the accuracy of what the first Christians proclaimed just a couple of years after Jesus' resurrection. They believed and recorded that he was the incarnate Son of God, a miracle worker who died and rose from the dead for the forgiveness of our sins. Paul tells us that many in the early church saw him and believed that his death and resurrection redeemed them from their sins. God, as it were, absorbed the effects of our sins so that we could be forgiven and live in freedom. We become more confident in these truths as we allow Jesus to transform our minds. This gives us more courage and confidence to defend our beliefs and share with others the gift that Jesus is for all people. The more we read and study these bedrock scriptures, the more convinced we become that Jesus truly is the divine Son of *Abba,* who died for our sins and is alive today. Because he is alive, we can experience him in our hearts and receive healing in his presence.

As we soak in these scriptures, our minds become transformed "so that we may judge what is God's will, what is good, pleasing, and perfect" (Romans 12:2). People often ask me, "When I take quiet time, how can I tell that it is God talking to me?" The first question is, "Does it sound like Jesus?" We will look through more of the bedrock scriptures in this chapter to discover what Jesus said. Jesus' words to us today will sound like what he said in the gospels. The more we read and absorb his words, the more we will be able to distinguish them from the words of the present age. We might also see how they are different from our own desires. Then, we are in a position to make a choice to either conform to the present age or to follow the divine words of Jesus. If we have not already, we will notice that the words of Jesus can be challenging and sometimes contrary to our desires; however, we will also discover that following Jesus' teachings brings immense joy to our heart and serenity within our being. We will notice that Jesus' words are never shaming. Jesus did not shame people. Jesus' words are not angry. They are compassionate, encouraging, and healing. If we begin by feeling God's love for us, as we did in the retreat, we will have the energy and willingness to submit to whatever Jesus says. By Jesus' grace and his love, we can make the journey to the transformation of our heart and mind.

It might be helpful to note that most scripture scholars believe Mark, the gospel writer, was the interpreter of Peter and his scribe (1 Peter 5:13). There are differing opinions, but the most plausible one is that Mark recorded stories told directly by Peter who was with Jesus for three years and experienced him alive after the resurrection. He saw the events and knew the heart of Jesus. There is also evidence that Mark traveled with the apostle Paul (2 Timothy 4:11 and Philemon 23). These things indicate that Mark's gospel forms the bedrock foundation of the Christian story. In addition, Mark's gospel contains a number of Aramaic words, which is the language spoken by Jesus. We reflected on one of those words in the retreat. It is the word *"Abba"* that Jesus spoke in the garden of Gethsemane (Mark 14:36). This seems to come directly from the lips of Jesus as he prayed to Father God. Other Aramaic words in Mark's gospel are, *"Talitha koum"* that he said to the girl whom he raised from the dead (Mark 5:41), and *"Ephphatha"* that he said to the deaf man when he opened his ears to hear (Mark 7:34). These things assure us that we are hearing first-hand words from the Master. This knowledge helps us discern what thoughts or promptings are coming from Jesus and which ones are coming from some other source. It also helps us stay grounded in the truth when someone tries to dissuade us from what Jesus said.

If we look at the bedrock scripture of Mark's gospel, we notice at the beginning of his ministry, Jesus said to the people, "Reform your lives and believe in the gospel" (Mark 1:15). Jesus welcomed all people and then called each one to repent. Jesus offered everyone the invitation to the fullness of life; if they wanted it, they were challenged to repent. Jesus was inclusive, but he also called everyone to make a change. The Greek word for reform or repent is *"metanoia."* It means to turn around and change the direction of your life. People had to let go of behaviors contrary to the teachings of Jesus. Today, many people use the word "inclusive" to mean that anyone can be a Christ follower and keep behaving like they did before. That is not what Jesus said. We read throughout the gospel that those who wanted to be disciples of Jesus had to *"metanoia."* They had to align their actions with the teachings of Jesus. Some chose to do so, and some did not. When we experience Jesus' deep love and wish to live in his presence, we are willing to do whatever he asks. Sometimes, our change may be gradual, but we choose to begin the transformation process.

In this same section, Mark wrote, "Jesus entered the synagogue and began to teach. The people were spellbound by his teaching because he taught with authority, and not like the scribes." (Mark 1:21–21). Jesus spoke with a unique kind of authority because he had a unique relationship with the Author. His words came from divine authority. It is interesting that the people noticed a significant difference between the one speaking with divine authority and those speaking from the authority of human selection and human study. It is important to study but also to submit that study to the divine authority for authenticity. We are only authorized to say what Jesus tells us to say. The disciples shared that authority by being committed to Jesus and his words. We also share in that authority by surrendering to Jesus' will in our words and actions.

In the story of the penitent woman (Luke 7:36–50), we read how repentance opens the door to receive Jesus' peace. Here, a woman who had done wrong came into the Pharisee's house where Jesus was and showed her repentant heart by washing and anointing Jesus' feet. She could share in the new life that Jesus gave while the Pharisee who did not repent remained judgmental and outside the circle of friendship which Jesus offered. The Pharisee and some of the religious leaders could not see their need to repent. All had an opportunity to repent, but unless they did, they would not enjoy the deep relationship that Jesus wanted for them. They did not receive the peace that Jesus offered. They needed to be humble enough to admit their need for repentance. We are each invited to that same humility and surrender.

This call to repent and change is portrayed in the gospels as changing garments. We see this in Mark's account of the blind beggar along the road (Mark 10:46–52). The blind man called out to Jesus, and when Jesus invited him over, he "threw aside his cloak." Clothing in the New Testament often represents a person's personality or way of life. This man was ready for a complete change. Once he received his sight, he followed Jesus up the road. This was the road to Jerusalem, where Jesus would be crucified. The man was ready to follow Jesus even up that road. He saw life in a new way and made a significant change.

This concept might help us understand what Jesus said about sewing a patch on a garment. Jesus said, "No one sews a patch of unshrunk cloth on an old cloak. If he should do so, the very thing he has used to cover the hole would pull away—the new from the old—and the tear would get worse" (Mark 2:21). Our bedrock scriptures tell us that being a Christian means not just adding a few "patches" to our life, but rather putting on a whole new garment. It means a change from thinking and acting in worldly ways to living as Jesus asks of us. We are called to be clothed in the values and ways of Jesus.

This image is also evident in the story of the man delivered from legions of demons (Mark 5:1–15). We read that he was found after his deliverance, sitting with Jesus, "fully clothed and in his right mind." Jesus' cleansing love gave him a new garment to wear. He had to choose it since demons cannot be expelled unless the host person chooses to participate in sending them out. With his new garment on, this man was empowered to return to his people and proclaim the saving message of Jesus.

The final image in Mark's gospel leaves us with the story of a "young man sitting in the tomb, dressed in a white robe" (Mark 16:5). This picture reminds us of the baptized person who threw off their old garment and is now dressed in a new white garment. He is sitting in all the signs of death yet proclaiming life because he has experienced the resurrection. He is like many early Christians who were surrounded by death but continued to proclaim new life because they had experienced Jesus as alive and were clothed in his love. All these images in this bedrock gospel affirm the total, life-changing commitment of the early Christians. They challenge us to choose the same life-giving relationship with Jesus. I have watched many Christians move from a mediocre commitment to Jesus to a life-changing commitment as they went through the six-week spiritual retreat described in chapter two. As adults, they had a chance to renew their baptism, surrender their lives completely to Jesus, and experience the healing love of the Holy Spirit. They became empowered disciples of Jesus and were ready to go out and make more disciples.

Everyone has to choose to change, to turn around, or to keep living as the world does. The apostle Paul, in his letter to the Ephesians, describes this necessary *metanoia* as well. He writes, "You must lay aside your former way of life and the old self which deteriorates through illusion and desire, and acquire a fresh, spiritual way of thinking. You must put on the new person created in God's image, whose justice and holiness are born of truth" (Ephesians

4:22–24). As Christians, we are called not to conform to the present culture but to be transformed in heart and mind. If we are going to be the "salt of the earth," as Jesus calls us to be, we must live differently than the world, to bring new flavor to our environment. This does not mean we may not falter at times, but we must turn back again and align ourselves with Jesus' teaching.

Mark gives us a glimpse of how Jesus could live with such peace and focus. He was empowered by the Father's love. The story of Jesus being transfigured offers a picture of what happened to Jesus when he went off alone and prayed (Mark 9:2–8). His garment, his personality, lit up with the fullness of the Father's love. At the transfiguration, he took his three main apostles along to experience the power of alone prayer time. Here is where he received his empowerment for ministry. Here also is where the Father affirms Jesus as his Son. We read, "A cloud came, overshadowing them, and out of the cloud a voice, 'This is my Son, my beloved. Listen to him.'" The Father reveals Jesus as his Son and tells the disciples to listen to him. This experience would have assured the disciples to follow Jesus wherever he led them. It is a message that we can all hear. When we take quiet, alone time in prayer, we can feel our insides light up with God's love and expect to hear Jesus speak to us.

As we continue to examine the bedrock scriptures, we recognize how unique Jesus' teachings and actions were compared to the messages of people of his time. His radical love for people empowered them to be healed physically, emotionally, and spiritually. He demonstrated an intense love that changed people's lives. He healed the sick, freed those possessed by evil, and forgave those who sought forgiveness. His love also invited and empowered people to change their behavior and love as he loved. All of this he did with his disciples watching him. His words and actions showed them the way to live the fullness of life.

Jesus' definition of love was what we call sacrificial love. He loved so deeply that he was willing to suffer for those he loved. He accepted ridicule for healing people. Ultimately, he knew he would be crucified for the message he brought to the world. Calling people to change offended some, yet he accepted the risk of death to bring people to the fullness of life. Jesus paid the price of his life to set people free of their destructive behavior. He wanted all to live as God intended. Because he loved so much, he could not silently watch as people defiled the life that he knew they were intended to have.

Mark's gospel records how Jesus came to realize that he would suffer ridicule and death for his teachings and actions, but he found a way to put meaning even in his suffering. He did not see his suffering as a sign of the end times or as a punishment from God. That is what his contemporaries would have done. Instead, he saw the suffering involved with his mission as redemptive, as beneficial for the people he had come to redeem. We find in our bedrock scriptures how Jesus saw himself as the Servant of God, described by the prophet Isaiah. This Servant accepted his sufferings as part of his mission to serve God. Jesus refers the servant sayings from Isaiah chapter 53 to himself in several places in Mark's gospel. We can read this in Mark 8:31 and 9:12 from Isaiah 53:3, the servant must suffer much; Mark 9:31 from Isaiah 53:5, be delivered over; Mark 10:45 and Mark 14:24 from Isaiah 53:11-12, for the salvation of many; Mark14:8 from Isaiah 53:9, be buried among criminals, without anointing; Mark 14:61 from Isaiah 53:7, and accept all this without opening his mouth. This fact that Jesus viewed his suffering as redemptive was significant to the early Christians. They were often persecuted, but this message from the Master allowed them to accept it as beneficial for the people they served. In Acts of the Apostles, we see that after the resurrection, the apostles were whipped for speaking about Jesus. Yet they were "full of joy that they had been judged worthy of ill-treatment for the sake of Jesus' name" (Acts 5:41). It may be hard to imagine that, but it speaks of a very deep love relationship between Jesus and his followers. This message is a source of encouragement for us when people respond negatively to us when we teach as Jesus taught and live the transformed life.

Jesus gave his disciples the new commandment to "love one another as I have loved you" (John 15:12). which is quite different than the old commandment to "love your neighbor as yourself." It is good to love our neighbors as we love ourselves, but to love them as Jesus loves us is a larger asking. Jesus' definition of love involves sacrifice. He was willing to die because he loved us so intensely. This differs from how the word *love* is often used in our world and even in our churches. It is often used to mean letting people do whatever they want so we do not offend them. When we love as Jesus has loved us, we recognize that it will involve sacrifice. It may be the sacrifice of accepting ridicule for speaking Jesus' truths to people in a world that does not accept them. It may be the challenge of letting go of our will to follow what Jesus asks of us. If we truly love people as Jesus loves us, we would not want them to live a destructive life pattern. We would invite them to the fullness of life that Jesus offers, even if it means risking the relationship.

Loving as Jesus loves us means opening ourselves to receiving Jesus' love. Jesus said, "As the Father loves me, so I love you" (John 15:9). If we take time often to ponder how much the Father loves Jesus and how much he loves us, then making a sacrifice for him is not too difficult. This is part of the transformed life that brings a deep joy to our hearts.

We also know that many people do not love themselves, and so loving their neighbor as they love themselves might not appear very loving. People abuse their bodies, cause themselves stress, and sometimes actually dislike what they have become. If they feel shameful about themselves, they will often shame other people. If they live with anger inside, they often take it out on those close to them. From such a perspective, they will not be inclined to treat their neighbor very well. As mentioned above, if we receive Jesus' deep love for us, it heals our hearts and changes how we view ourselves. This makes it possible for us to love others as Jesus loves us. This is the fruit of being transformed by the renewal of our mind. Inviting Jesus into our life empowers us to love as he did.

It is very interesting to note that Jesus' way of loving changed even those who did not know him. In the core gospel, we read that Jesus even changed people's lives by the way he died. Mark wrote in his gospel, "The centurion who stood guard over Jesus, on seeing the manner of his death, declared, 'Clearly this man was the

Son of God'" (Mark 15:39). This centurion was a Roman who did not know anything about Jesus except to watch the way he faced death. He saw first-hand the power of Divine love. It is recorded that many non-believers in Rome in the first centuries of Christianity were changed when they witnessed the early Christians ministering to the lepers in the city. They saw this unique group of people who were not afraid to die to bring healing and salvation to those in need. They watched some of these Christians get killed for their belief in Jesus. They accepted death like the Master because of their commitment to follow him and love as he loved them. Peter and Paul accepted this same fate, and many likely witnessed their sacrifice for Jesus. Stephen was killed for proclaiming the message of Jesus, and it is recorded that the apostle Paul watched him die. I believe this began Paul's transformation to a life committed to Jesus. In Paul's letters, we read that he handled his persecution and scourging by uniting his suffering to that of Jesus.

Getting beaten, ridiculed, or dismissed is not fun for anyone. However, our bedrock scriptures tell us it is sometimes part of living our Christian witness. In our time, when faithful Christians are being persecuted for proclaiming the gospel message, the witness of Jesus and the first believers can be a source of encouragement and joy. We may not get beaten or risk death for our faith, but if we are going to live a transformed life and not conform to this age, we will get some persecution or ridicule. For this reason, it is essential to reflect on our core scriptures and soak in Jesus' love daily. By the power of that love, we can continue his ministry, offer truth to our world, and demonstrate the power of his love.

The joy of being very closely connected to Jesus and the Father is that we can live each day in total serenity, immersed in the perfect love that created us. We can feel this awesome love every morning when we wake up and throughout the day. We can feel protection and power to heal and handle situations that might otherwise hurt us. We can feel like we are walking in our true identity and destiny, empowered by divine love. Jesus said, "As the Father has loved me, so I have loved you" (John 15:9). Living in that atmosphere of divine love gives us the strength to handle any challenges that may come along. That is why we turn our lives around; the new life is so much richer than the life of the world.

Our bedrock scriptures give us some foundational teachings of Jesus that help us handle the many messages in our culture. In Mark's gospel, chapter 10, verse 6–9, we read Jesus' definition of marriage. He said, "At the beginning of creation, God made them male and female; for this reason, a man shall leave his father and mother and the two shall become as one. They are no longer two but one flesh." It is essential to understand what Jesus said since we live in a world where all kinds of unions are being called "marriage." Jesus taught that only one type of union is a marriage. He roots marriage in God's intention for creation. God created them male and female to image the divine. When both are joined in love, they become a picture of God's masculine and feminine love on earth. That is why it is such a unique and special union. No other unions do that. People can have various friendships and commitments, but only one man and one woman can be a picture of God's love and can be co-creators of life with God. Only the two together can be the agents for creating life as God wills. Early in Christian history, the community took special care to nurture these unique relationships. They desired to have images of God's love in their communities. They treasured these unique relationships.

We also recognize that only a man and a woman can create the environment of masculine and feminine love in which a child can grow and come to understand what it means to be a man or woman. It is no wonder that with the destruction of healthy marriages in our culture, so many children are mixed up about their sexual identity. I once heard Bill Jarema talk about the father wound. He said that the father's love gives a child the container, and the mother's love gives a child the fluid for the container. These are generalizations, but from my experience, it is often a healthy father who provides a child with a strong identity and a healthy mother who teaches the child how to express their feelings and share intimately. Jesus knew that healthy marriages were crucial to raising well-formed children. It is difficult to watch how our society is destructive to such families. It is saddening to see how some churches are participating in this process. We need to affirm marriage as Jesus defined it and foster healthy marriages and families.

In this passage, Jesus also speaks about divorce. He rejects the Pharisee's way of allowing divorce for convenience. He taught that marriages were to be "joined by God." Statistics show that when a man and a woman feel God's deep love and share that love with each other, their marriage is much more likely to last. Feeling God's love is a powerful force in keeping two people together. They share not only their human love but they share God's love with each other that heals and brings peace. This gift helps them to forgive, share, and let go of personal gain at times for the benefit of the other. It also helps them hear the other person's pain instead of reacting to their painful words or actions. This healing and forgiving love makes it possible for a marriage to last a lifetime. When God does not join two people in marriage, it does not always last. Jesus spoke of forgiveness and, in the case of a broken marriage, people need to ask for forgiveness, make amends, and then move on. They need to repent and begin again to live in the beauty of Jesus' mercy and love.

Another exciting facet of Jesus' teaching in our bedrock scriptures is how Jesus gave personhood to all people. This may not be as well-known as other teachings, but it is very significant regarding how we treat people. In an article entitled "Human Dignity Was a Rarity Before Christianity," David Bentley Hart makes the case that Jesus was revolutionary in affirming the dignity of every person. He writes that the notion of every person having innate human worth came about only as the "consequence of a cultural, moral revolution that erupted with Christianity."

David goes on to say that this revolution is evident in the story of Peter weeping after he betrayed Jesus (Mark 14:72). We expect Peter to weep, but this is not how the contemporaries of Mark would have seen it. He says, "To call attention to Peter's grief would have seemed like a mistake, for Peter, a rustic peasant from Galilee, could not possibly have been a worthy subject of a well-born man's sympathy, nor could his sorrow possibly have possessed the sort of tragic dignity necessary to make it a suitable subject of an historian." He writes that "tragic dignity was the exclusive property of the well born," and Peter was not of that class. This may be hard for us to understand, but in these ancient times, personhood was only assigned to those who held status before the law. The greater number of people were classified as "not persons." These included Peter, the other disciples, and even Jesus. David points out that giving Peter the dignity to call attention to his weeping was not a mere mistake by Mark, but it was an "act of rebellion." He goes on to say that for the first time in human history, the human person was invested with an intrinsic worth, an infinite value. This revolution happened because Jesus taught that each person came from the Father, not from any particular geographic area. Their dignity was from being a child of God. David writes, "For us to give personhood to everyone we meet is the consequence of this Jesus-led revolution. It is practically impossible for us today to appreciate the magnitude of the scandal that many pagans naturally felt at the bizarre way the early Christians were willing to grant full humanity to persons of every class and condition."

Once we understand how revolutionary Jesus was in this regard, we appreciate even more how Jesus could stand before Pilate with such peace. He knew he came from the Father and was going back to the Father. He stood in the power of the Father's deep love for him. He stood in divine dignity, as we can do. The people of his time would have considered him to have no personhood. They thought he was from Galilee, which gave him no recognition before the law, but Jesus knew he was from the Father with all the dignity of God's Son. The people would have thought of Jesus as having no power, but his resurrection caused "the great reversal of power, the revolution of personhood." Personhood was now recognized as coming from one's true origins, from God. This could explain why Peter and John could stand before the Sanhedrin and not back down from teaching Jesus' message. They knew their origin (Acts 4:13–21). They had been healed by being in Jesus' presence and emboldened by his example.

When people discover their true identity and dignity comes from the Father, they have an inner strength and peace that no one can take away. The power for ministry flows from their true identity and origin. This is all found in our bedrock scriptures. Our Christian communities need leaders who teach as Jesus taught with that kind of inner strength, leaders who have received inner healing and do not give in to the pressures of the culture. Christian communities today need courageous leaders who are ready to accept any ridicule or persecution they receive for being faithful to the message that Jesus proclaimed, leaders who demonstrate his compassion and the healing power of his love.

Jesus gave equal dignity to all persons because they are all created in the love of the Father, Son, and Holy Spirit. In Mark's chapter on marriage, we see how Jesus gave equal dignity to men and women. He says that both are equally responsible for caring for the needs of the other. This was a unique teaching for his time and remains an important message today. This section also shows that Jesus affirms children as having full personhood and are to be treated with love. Children at that time were not supposed to interrupt a Rabbi like Jesus, but Jesus said, "Let the children come to me" (Mark 10:14). He then embraced and blessed them. As we reflect on these core scriptures, we might consider the unborn children who do not have full personhood in our culture and who do not have any rights before the law. They get destroyed and thrown in the garbage. This is not in keeping with Jesus' "revolution of personhood." They are the Father's unique creations and have personhood as his daughters and sons. We cannot be conformed to this age and still stand with Jesus.

One further teaching of Jesus found in our bedrock scriptures is a list of behaviors that defile a person and make a person impure. Jesus said, "Wicked designs come from the deep recesses of the heart; acts of fornication (sexual acts outside of marriage as Jesus defined it), theft, murder, adulterous conduct, greed, maliciousness, deceit, sensuality, envy, blasphemy, arrogance, and lewdness. All these evils come from within and render a person impure" (Mark 7:21–23). As people seeking to live transformed lives, we need to root such behaviors out of our lives. They tear away at a healthy life and separate us from our Creator. We must decide to repent as Jesus asks us to do. We are all human and can falter at times, but this is about recognizing these as defiling behaviors and making an intentional decision to change. The Christian community cannot bless such behaviors; instead, it is called to help people turn away from destructive behaviors. This begins by helping people to receive God's deep love for them and establishing a desire to change. By the power of his creative, healing love, we can transform our lives. This is a power that the culture does not know. Conforming to its ways does not help anyone. Christians are called to be transformed by the renewal of their minds and hearts. Living a transformed life gives us the energy to change ourselves and walk with those who also wish to live the fullness of life.

Jesus desires that we live in the joy and peace of his presence and offer his healing love to all people. I worked with a man who was caught up in homosexual acts. As he heard me talk about God's immense love for him and how feeling that love could bring about inner healing and healing of the father wound, he kept coming to hear more. He attended several healing services and gradually started pulling away from his homosexual activity. He thanked me often for offering him the way and the power to get free. He made progress, but sadly, before he got totally free, he contracted AIDs. Even on his deathbed, he thanked me for introducing him to Jesus' healing love.

There are other important messages that we find in the bedrock scriptures. In his gospel, Mark notes the difference between being cured and being made whole. He records that Jesus could cure (in Greek, *etherapoisen*) a few people in Nazareth, but he could not make them well because they lacked faith (Mark 6:5). In Mark 5:25–34, he records how the woman with the flow of blood believed that if she touched the garment of Jesus, she would be made whole *(sothesomai)*. At the end of the account, Jesus said, "Daughter, your faith has made you well *(sesoken)*." It did not take faith to be cured by Jesus. His intense love for a person could cure them. However, if they wanted to be well, they needed to enter into a faith relationship with him. That was their decision to commit their lives to him. That decision would make them well forever. This is true today, also. Jesus' healing ministry was part of bringing people to an eternal faith relationship with him. Those open to such a commitment would begin living a transformed life with an eternal destiny. This story dovetails with our reflection about putting on the new garment. The woman reached out to touch Jesus' garment, which can also mean touching the life of Jesus. By touching his life, his personality changed and healed her. In chapter 6, verse 56, we read how many people sought to touch the garment of Jesus. It says, "All who touched him were made whole." Spiritual wholeness and wellness come from "touching the garment of Jesus" every day. It is about accepting his way of life.

This early bedrock account has ramifications for Christians today. It informs us that if someone is not cured of a disease, it does not mean they lack faith. It can mean that no one is helping them to feel God's deep love for them, or they have some blocks to feeling God's love. They may need to forgive someone. They may need a new picture of God given to us by Jesus. Maybe they need to be soaked in a healing environment for a longer period to break through several inner wounds which need healing. They may need to release repressed emotions that are affecting their physical condition. And sometimes, we do not know why a specific cure does not happen, but we are still called to pray for healing as part of proclaiming the message of Jesus. Offering the profound love of Jesus to someone always brings about healing on some level.

This account also tells us that healing ministry is an essential part of proclaiming the gospel of Jesus. Christian churches must reinstate this ministry into their teachings if they desire to do what Jesus did. If we are to live a transformed life, the healing ministry, as Jesus shows us, is an essential part of that life. The healing ministry was almost completely lost throughout Christian history. We can read about this in Dr. Francis MacNutt's book, *The Healing Reawakening: Reclaiming Our Lost Inheritance*. It is being restored by people who have opened themselves to the full power of the Holy Spirit. Some places and groups train people in offering Jesus' healing presence to others. *Christian Healing Ministries* in Jacksonville Florida, is one of those places. *The International Order of St. Luke the Physician* and *The Association of Christian Therapists* are two organizations that train and support people in offering the healing power of Jesus to others. There are medical doctors and therapists in these organizations who pray with their patients in addition to using their learned skills. They see much greater health results using the additional power of God's healing love. We cannot just conform to what the world offers. We are called to be the salt of the earth, to bring a different flavor to the challenges of life. We must make available the gift that Jesus brought to the world by his life, death, and resurrection.

There is an interesting thing in Mark's gospel that can be confusing. We read that occasionally after Jesus cured someone, he told them not to tell anyone. We see this in the story of Jesus curing the deaf mute (Mark 7:31–37). It may look as if Jesus wanted to keep some secret and that does not make sense. If we look closely, we discover that Jesus asked people to be quiet about the cure until they were ready to be made whole. If they just talked about the cure, they would miss the essence of Jesus' message. He cured them as part of the greater miracle that he came to give, namely, wholeness, the fullness of life that lasts forever. When people decided to enter into a faith relationship, a faith commitment to him, they were encouraged to go and proclaim what he had done for them.

We read about the same concept in Mark, chapter 1, verses 24–25. There, Jesus tells the devil to be silent. The devil knew who Jesus was but was not committed to him. Knowing who Jesus is does not bring wholeness or salvation. We have seen that repenting or turning our lives around (*metanoia*) puts us in a position to enter into a lifelong relationship with Jesus. Then, we are ready to proclaim his message.

There is an underlying message in chapter 13 of Mark's gospel that is encouraging and clarifying when we hear talk about the end of the world. In this chapter, Mark records Jesus predicting the destruction of Jerusalem and some words about a second coming. The main message of this chapter is that not even Jesus knew when the second coming would happen. If Jesus did not know, it is unlikely that anyone else knows, even if they say they do. People sometimes talk about the end of the world to scare others into changing their lives. Jesus did not use fear to change people; rather, he offered his sacrificial love to call them to change. He called people to remain faithful to him and continue his ministry so they would be ready to go home to the Father whenever it was time.

One last important message we discover in the bedrock scriptures that empowers Christians to live a transformed life is an early understanding of the Last Supper. This core understanding of the Last Supper has ramifications for celebrating the Eucharist today (Mark 14:12–25). Mark records an interesting statement in his Last Supper account that is not found in the other gospels. We read, "During the meal, Jesus took bread, blessed and broke it, and gave it to them. 'Take this,' he said, 'this is my body.' He likewise took the cup, gave thanks, and passed it to them, and they all drank from it. He said to them, 'This is my blood of the new covenant, to be poured out on behalf of many.'" I want to point specifically to the statement, "They all drank from it." No other gospel records that. What is Mark trying to say with those words? I think we can understand it if we recall Jesus' question to James and John when they asked earlier if they could sit at Jesus' right and left in the kingdom. Jesus asked them, "Can you drink the cup I shall drink or be baptized in the same bath of pain as I?" (Mark 10:38) So, when Mark records this unique statement, "They all drank from it," he indicates that Jesus was not only committing his body and blood to the disciples at the Last Supper, but they were committing their body and blood to him by drinking from the cup. It was a meal with a double commitment. Jesus called it a covenant, which means that each side offered something. The disciples were affirming their commitment to stay with Jesus and accept whatever challenges that would entail. Their commitment was in response to Jesus' commitment to them.

Mark's account of the preparation for the Last Supper affirms this same understanding. The disciple's question to Jesus, "Where do you wish us to go to prepare the Passover for *you*?" indicates that they think the meal was for Jesus. Jesus gives them directions and then says, "That is the place you are to get ready for *us*" (Mark 14:12–16). The meal was for all of them. Jesus was going to draw them into a covenant relationship with him that night which they could continue to feel every time they broke bread in memory of him after that. They also committed their lives to each other as they all drank from the cup. That gesture bonded them in a new way.

This understanding of the Last Supper helps us comprehend why celebrating the Eucharist was central to the early church. At their baptism, the early Christians made a total life commitment to Jesus, and then every Saturday evening or Sunday, they would renew that commitment in the Eucharist. In this time of persecution, the continual remembering of Jesus' sacrifice for them empowered them to renew their commitment to sacrifice for him.

Before I was ordained to the priesthood, a retreat director pointed out this original understanding of the Eucharist. He said that when we, as priests, celebrate the Eucharist, if we only repeat the words of Jesus, we are not celebrating the Eucharist. To celebrate the Eucharist meant to recommit ourselves to Jesus and the people in our community as the early Christians did. That gave every Eucharistic celebration a much deeper meaning for me. As I shared this understanding with my communities, they began to realize that they, too, made a commitment to Jesus and to the community each time they celebrated Eucharist. In response to Jesus' gift of himself to us, we said, "Thank you, and this is my body and my blood for you." People spontaneously started saying the blessing prayer with me because they wanted to feel themselves giving their "yes" at this commitment meal. This understanding brought our community much closer together and empowered us for ministry.

It is an unfortunate thing that the Christian church lost this bedrock understanding of the Eucharist. By the fifth century, the church took on a more political flavor, and this original meaning of the Eucharist became overshadowed by people's desire to receive without the commitment to give. By the Middle Ages, the Eucharist was more of a show with vestments and pageantry. Many renewal movements discarded it completely. That is why many denominations do not celebrate the Eucharist today. If Christian churches are going to be salt for the world, they would do well to rediscover the core meaning of the Eucharist. If Christians are going to "be transformed by the renewal of their mind and heart," they need to seek a way of celebrating the Eucharist in its original, powerful form. They need a place to recommit their body and blood to the mission of Jesus at the beginning of every week.

All of these teachings are part of our bedrock scriptures. They are recorded so soon after Jesus' life, death, and resurrection that they demonstrate clear evidence of who he was as God's Son and what his coming to earth has meant for all humanity. They contain the fundamental teachings and attitudes of Jesus before philosophies and political influences altered them. They contain the basis of our Christian faith. These scriptures are essential to renewing our minds "so that we may judge what is God's will, what is good, pleasing and perfect." In our quiet time and in our ministry, these words guide our choices and teachings.

Prayer of Gratitude

Jesus, I thank you for coming to earth, revealing the Father's love for me, and demonstrating your sacrificial love. You made great sacrifices to offer healing and life-giving teachings to our world. You taught me the healthiest way to live. You empower me to change my human ways so I can walk in your divine ways. You have shown me how to live a life of serenity and joy. You have demonstrated how to resist temptation and destructive choices, so I might feel deeply connected to you and your Father. Thank you, Jesus, for your message and the power to live it. Thank you for inviting me to the meal that nourishes my deepest needs and keeps me connected to you and the Eucharistic community. Jesus, you are a treasure, and I love you. Amen.

Questions

Which teachings of Jesus were new to you?

Which teachings offer the greatest challenge to you?

How can knowing the core teachings of Jesus help you share your
faith with others?

CHAPTER 5

Completing the Picture of Jesus

In addition to the bedrock scriptures, the gospels of Matthew, Luke, and John inform us about Jesus and a transformed life. These gospels were written during the decades following Mark's gospel and include his material plus additional stories that add to the description of Jesus. Each of these accounts demonstrates the unique life and ministry of Jesus, and each affirms that he is the Son of God who died and rose from the dead. His teachings and healing ministry reveal that he had divine power. His words tell us that he did not conform to the culture but was guided by the direction of the Father. He said, "I say only what the Father has taught me" (John 8:28). He only did what the Father directed him to do even when it meant suffering and ultimately led to his death. We can explore some of the divine treasures that Jesus received from the Father.

The gospel of Matthew includes many of the stories found in Mark, but the author adds some important teachings that enrich our understanding of Jesus' heart. The author of this gospel is writing for Jewish converts; therefore, it retains more of the heritage from which Jesus' family came. It explains Jesus in light of the Jews' expectation of the Messiah and how Jesus fulfilled that role. It offers a slightly different view of Jesus but still affirms his divinity and the treasures of his teaching.

One of the unique messages in Matthew's gospel is Jesus sharing the eight Beatitudes (Matthew 5:3–12). These words of Jesus reveal the attitudes and behaviors that bring true blessing and joy to a person. Jesus said that the people are blessed who are "poor in spirit." These are the ones who know they need God. He said that those who hunger and thirst for holiness will have their fill. Those who show mercy will receive mercy themselves. Those who may suffer persecution or ridicule for living a holy life will receive their reward. Jesus not only taught this, but he also lived this teaching. The followers of Jesus could find great comfort in these Beatitudes, and they remain a source of guidance and empowerment for us. They are not necessarily easy to follow, but they are possible by the power of God's Spirit. This teaching describes the transformed life which brings deep joy to those who live it.

Another text about Jesus found in Matthew's gospel are his compassionate words, "Come to me, you who are weary and find life burdensome, and I will refresh you. Take my yoke upon your shoulders and learn from me, for I am gentle and humble of heart. Your souls will find rest, for my yoke is easy, and my burden is light" (Matthew 11:28–29). Jesus knew that the human life journey could wear a person down, so he offered refreshment for the journey by inviting us to accept his way of life, which is much lighter. He assures us that if we are listening to him and surrendering our way of doing things, we will have him as a partner to lighten the burden. The yoke is used to connect two people, meaning that we then never walk alone. This statement gives a deep sense of joy, especially to those who feel a heavy weight in life. Jesus forgives our sins and heals our wounds, which lightens our load. He walks beside us and even carries us through the hardest times. He only asks that we surrender to him and allow him to walk with us to our created destiny.

At the end of his gospel, Matthew records Jesus' great commission to his followers. Their commitment to him meant they were given a charge and the authority to carry it out. Jesus said, "Full authority has been given to me both in heaven and on earth. Go, therefore, and make disciples of all the nations. Baptize them in the name of the Father, and the Son, and the Holy Spirit. Teach them to carry out everything I have commanded you. And know that I am with you always, until the end of the world" (Matthew 28:18–29). We have the authority of Jesus to teach as he taught, but it is important to understand that we do not have the authority to teach what he did not teach. Renewing our minds includes studying what Jesus said and did so that our teaching and behavior are accurate. We cannot modify his teaching to fit the culture. We are commissioned to offer the pure teaching of Jesus to the culture with the hopes of leading some to baptism into life with him. This is a formidable challenge in a time when there are many messages about Jesus in the air. Looking at the bedrock scriptures and surrendering our lives to Jesus gives us a solid foundation from which to teach and act. We are called to make disciples, but we can only make them if we are empowered by the Holy Spirit and speaking from the solid foundation of Jesus' teachings. Also found in these words is the great assurance that Jesus will always be with us, surrounding us in his love.

The gospel of Luke is written not long after the bedrock scriptures of Mark and Paul's letters. Luke was a physician, a learned man who set out to give a comprehensive account of the life of Jesus. He knew and traveled with Mark and Paul (2 Timothy 4:11). He begins his gospel by saying, "Many have undertaken to compile a narrative of the events which have been fulfilled in our midst, precisely as those events were transmitted to us by the original eyewitnesses and ministers of the word. I, too, have carefully traced the whole sequence of events from the beginning, and have decided to set it in writing for you, friend of God, so that you may see how reliable the instruction was that you received" (Luke 1:1–4). Luke adds many more details about the life of Jesus, which helps complete our picture of him and allows us to see his compassionate heart. Luke also wrote Acts of the Apostles, which gives us a picture of the Christian community's growth after Jesus' resurrection.

One of the first things we notice in Luke's gospel is his recording of the commission Jesus felt for his life. At the beginning of his ministry, Jesus read from the prophet Isaiah, "The Spirit of the

Lord is upon me; therefore, he has anointed me. He has sent me to bring glad tidings to the poor, to proclaim liberty to captives, recovery of sight to the blind and release to prisoners, to announce a year of favor from the Lord" (Luke 4:18–19). Jesus read his scriptures and heard the Father's word through them. He discerned his mission and then began to carry it out. Jesus modeled how to get instructions and receive the anointing to move in the power of the Spirit. He was to bring hope to the poor, heal those in need, release those imprisoned within themselves, and announce God's favor toward all people. We read how he carried out this mission throughout the gospel by living the transformed life and inviting all who desired this fullness of life to walk with him.

The bedrock scriptures of Mark were available to Luke, and he repeats many of the stories told there, but he adds some of his own. One of his unique stories is the account of the Good Samaritan (Luke 10:25–37). He records Jesus defining what it means to be a neighbor in God's worldview. He says the Samaritan was "moved with compassion" for the injured man along the road. That phrase in scripture was used to describe the heart of Jesus. When Jesus saw someone in need of healing, he was "moved with compassion" and healed them. In this story, the Samaritan does the same and brings about healing. Jesus calls his disciples to be moved with compassion for those who are hurting and to reach out with his healing and saving power. That is the ministry of the Christian community. That is part of the transformed life.

Luke also adds the story of the prodigal son (Luke 15:10–32). Jesus tells the story to show the religious leaders of the time why he gathered together with sinners. He wanted to give a picture of the depth of God's mercy. The father in the story waits for his estranged son to come home. When he does, the father is overjoyed and has a banquet to celebrate. It portrays the joy of God when people repent and change their lives to be with him. In his book, *The Prodigal Father*, Timothy Keller points out an interesting thing about this story. He notes that both sons needed repentance: the younger one for doing the wrong thing and the older one for doing the right thing for the wrong reason. By the end of the story, we read how the older son would not go into the celebration. He was angry that the father had given away his cloak and killed the fatted calf. He stayed home the whole time and worked, not because he loved his father but because he wanted his father's possessions. That would have been his cloak and some of his money that the younger son had taken. Both sons only wanted the father's goods and both needed to repent. The younger son "came to his senses" and repented, but the older son was not ready to repent for his motive in staying home. He could not enjoy the celebration of repentance and forgiveness.

Everyone is welcome to the divine community, and everyone has to repent. We each need to be radically honest with ourselves. We need to be transformed by the renewal of our mind to live as God desires and let go of worldly ways and motives. Jesus said, "Repent and believe the good news." Entering into a relationship with Jesus means leaving behind what is incompatible with his message. When we do this, the deep joy of God wells up inside of us.

Luke is the only writer who records Jesus forgiving those who crucified him (Luke 23:34). This unique line in his gospel speaks loudly of Jesus' love for all people. His heart did not hold a grudge. He forgave those who killed him. Forgiving someone who has harmed us is one of the most difficult things to do, yet not forgiving is the most destructive thing we can hold inside. This example of Jesus on the cross must have influenced the early Christians and is an inspiration for us. We recognize that not forgiving someone does not hurt them, but it holds us in a prison of our own making. Releasing them releases us. The renewal of our mind opens us to this awareness and empowers us to forgive as Jesus forgave.

The last two stories only recorded by Luke in his gospel are the accounts of the two disciples on the road to Emmaus after Jesus' resurrection and Jesus eating with the eleven apostles after his resurrection (Luke 24:13–49). These are two clear accounts of Jesus being alive after his death. Again, these accounts were written when some eyewitnesses of these happenings were still alive. These disciples would see many more miracles, which are recorded by Luke in Acts of the Apostles.

The last of the four gospels was written about a decade later by John. Because the first three gospels were already known and read during the weekend worship, John does not repeat the stories told in them but offers some new accounts plus adds thoughts on the deeper meaning of Jesus' life and ministry. He opens his gospel with the words, "In the beginning was the Word; the Word was in God's presence, and the Word was God." (John 1:1). He is not concerned about the physical birth of Jesus, but rather, he affirms the divinity of Jesus. John attempts to describe the mystery of Jesus as being both God and human. As God, Jesus participated in creating all things, and then he became flesh "that the world might be saved through him" (John 3:16–17). His presence on earth, culminating with his death and resurrection, made it possible for us to be transformed and live in the world but not be of the world. He came that we "might have life, and have it to the full" (John 10:10).

John records an account of Jesus speaking with Nicodemus, telling him he must be born from above or be born again (John 3:1–16). His words describe the transformation that brings a person into a lifelong relationship with Jesus. It describes the person who gets instructions from above rather than from the world. It is what Paul calls *putting on the mind of Christ*. It is what we practiced in the retreat: quieting ourselves every day and listening for the messages God has for us. It is the interior decision to change the source of our instructions in life and follow what Jesus asks of us. This transforms our mind and heart and allows us to live life to the fullest.

In this gospel, we also find the story of the healing of the man born blind (John 9:1–38). In this account, Jesus dismissed the Jewish notion that God punished people by giving them blindness or an illness. Jesus used this occasion to have the man wash his eyes in the pool of Siloam, and in doing so, the man received his sight and an insight into who Jesus was. Jesus cured him as part of bringing him into a new way of understanding who he was and how he could live the fullness of life. The man made a commitment to follow Jesus and got badgered by his religious leaders about that commitment. They tried to dissuade him about the authenticity of

Jesus, but he felt the love, the power from above, and no one could change his mind about Jesus. He had been healed physically, emotionally, and spiritually. Even getting thrown out of his church did not deter him from following the one person who opened his eyes to real life. Everyone had treated him as a sinner to that point, but from now on he knew he was a son of the Father, a disciple of the Son. He would follow Jesus anywhere. He would live differently because now he saw life in a new way and understood himself in a new way. His instructions would come from above. It is a beautiful story of transformation.

Another story that is not told in the other three gospels is the account of the raising of Lazarus from the dead (John 11:1–46). We read that Jesus waited after hearing the news about Lazarus' illness. He ministered in the Father's timing, not his own. Then, he risked his life to go to Bethany and perform this miracle because giving life to others was more important than his own needs. We read further that when he got close to the tomb of Lazarus, "Jesus wept." He revealed his human heart that hurt, a heart that was moved with compassion when he saw others hurting. His tears tell us that it is all right to cry and that feeling someone else's pain is part of being a minister of healing. Being transformed does not alleviate all pain but puts us in a position to see the joy and benefits of surrendering all to God. Jesus looked up to heaven. He turned to the Father to proclaim from where all life-giving, healing energy comes. Next, we read how he called Lazarus to come out, and "the dead man (Lazarus) came out." If we only see a man physically walking out of the grave, then we miss the deeper meaning of this story. Jesus had described himself as the Good Shepherd. He said, "The sheep hear his voice as he calls his own by name. He walks in front of them, and the sheep follow him because they recognize his voice" (John 10:3–4). Lazarus heard the voice of Jesus, the Good Shepherd, and followed it. Now, he was transformed. He would live forever connected to Jesus. He went from having life, through death, to having a life that lasts forever. He received the fullness of life in Jesus. The voice of the Good Shepherd calls us out of the places where we do not have life and offers us life in abundance that has eternal significance.

This story offers deep healing to those who ponder it and listen to the voice of Jesus. We mentioned in chapter three how the voice of Jesus brings healing today. These words invite us to take Jesus to the "tombs" in our life where we have buried unresolved grief. We can listen to his voice and allow him to draw new life out of memories where we have experienced losses without fully processing our grief. We can feel Jesus cry with us and bring the Father's love to fill the place where the loss has left us empty. As we allow Jesus to help us resolve our grief, we prepare ourselves to help others do the same. Jesus' words, "Untie him and let him go free" (John 11:44), then have new meaning for us. This is the joy of being transformed by the renewal of our mind and heart. Our load is lightened, and our heart is refreshed.

Jesus' teachings and practice showed that he did not conform to the present age. He did as the Father guided him to do. John records the story of Jesus washing his disciple's feet (John 13:1–15). Such an act was only done by the servants in that culture. Jesus wanted his disciples to know that he was willing to serve them so that they would know they were cleansed. He also gave them an example of how they were to serve others. Interestingly, John writes, "Jesus, fully aware that he had come from the Father and was going back to the Father," began to wash his disciple's feet. Knowing his true identity, origin, and destiny allowed him to do this menial task without feeling diminished in any way. When we recognize our self-worth as daughters and sons of the Father, we can serve in any way God asks of us. We do not need worldly recognition. We need only to remember to whom we truly belong.

John leaves us one last treasure. In chapters 14–17, he records Jesus' final conversation with his apostles. Slowly reading through those chapters gives us a beautiful picture of Jesus' heart. His tender words to his disciples allow us to feel his tender love for us. He said, "Do not let your hearts be troubled. Have faith in God and faith in me. In my Father's house there are many dwelling places; otherwise, how could I have told you that I was going to prepare a place for you. I am indeed going to prepare a place for you, and then I will come back and take you with me, that where I am you might also be" (John 14:1–3). His words tell us of his deep love and desire to have us where he is. He continues, "As the Father has loved me, so I have loved you, live on in my love" (John 15:9). Imagine how intensely the Father loves Jesus and then stop and bask in that love. The magnitude of that love is awesome beyond our imagination, yet there it is for us to receive.

Jesus then continues with his new commandment, "Love one another as I have loved you" (John 15:12). His love is so strong that he sacrifices his life for us. Even though he challenges his followers to love with this kind of love, it is possible because his love empowers us. We surrender our will because living in his love brings joy and peace that the world cannot give. It transforms our minds and hearts to see life from his perspective. Living his destiny for our lives offers us excitement about what the next calling will be. It gives us inner security and greater self-esteem knowing we are walking in the purpose of our Creator. We can feel his continuing love because he has called us "friends." This is much greater than worldly recognition. Feeling that friendship bond makes us want to do the right thing, not because we have to but because we want to please our Friend. We do not work for his love but from his love. We talk with him often to enrich the friendship. We worship him often to honor our friend and thank him for his precious love. Living this way is the fullness of life, the transformed life.

In the following verses, Jesus says, "If you find that the world hates you, know that it has hated me before you. If you belong to the world, it would love you as its own; the reason it hates you is that you do not belong to the world. I chose you out of the world" (John 15:18–19). There can be a price for not conforming to the cultural values. If we live and teach Jesus' message, some people will be offended, but they were offended by Jesus also. The friendship with Jesus is more valuable than the acceptance of the world. We do not offend people with harsh words, insensitivity, or rash judgements, but we may offend people by being true to Jesus' words. Jesus "offended" people to bring them out of themselves and invite them to the fullness of life.

Then, we hear Jesus' final prayer for his disciples and us. He prayed, "Father, for these I pray, not for the world, but for these you have given me, for they are really yours. . . I do not pray for them alone. I pray also for those who will believe in me through their words, that all may be one as you, Father, are in me and I am in you; I pray that they may be one in us" (John 17:9, 20–21). Jesus prayed for his disciple' protection and for them to remain connected to him. He also prays for us who believe. He prays that we will be one with him, taking in his energy daily and feeling the joy of our unity with him. He does not pray for unity with the world but for the profound unity with him. He makes it clear that Christians are called out of the world to stand in his truth, to bring a divine worldview to those of the world. He says, "I consecrate myself for their sake now, that they may be consecrated in truth" (John 17:19). He has given his life so that we might know what the truth is and might have the courage to stand with him in proclaiming the truth of real life. Knowing Jesus prays for us is a tremendous source of strength, especially in challenging times. We never stand alone.

These and other stories and words in the gospels give us a beautiful picture of Jesus and his deep care for all people. They show us a God-man who continually loved and revealed the power of divine love. They draw us into the heart of God and refresh the part of us that knows we need God. Absorbing these words allows us to experience our Friend and enjoy his compassionate heart.

Prayer for a Heart of Compassion

Jesus, you gave me so many stories to get to know your heart of compassion. You demonstrated a heart that felt deep sadness and a heart that was moved when someone was hurting. In your ministry, you demonstrated a true care for people and a desire to set them free. You wanted to protect your followers and assure them that you would always remain with them. Jesus, let me feel your heart of love every day. Pour your immense love into me so I will overflow with love and compassion for every person I meet. Give me the courage and compassion to live out your divine commission for my life. Let me hear your direction from above and be empowered to walk every day in your will. Thank you for assuring me of your presence with me always. Amen.

Questions

Which gospel stories most speak to your heart?

Has any of these stories broadened your picture of Jesus and the Father?

What does it mean to you that Jesus prays for you?

CHAPTER 6

The First Transformed Christian Community

We get a picture of what Jesus' words and presence did for those early disciples as we look at Acts of the Apostles. This book tells us about those who followed Jesus after his resurrection and how they made his message understandable to those who wished to live like him. We find significant evidence of the transforming power of the Holy Spirit. Not only did many people see Jesus alive after his resurrection, but they felt his living presence within themselves. They were ready to do whatever he asked of them. This apostolic witness makes the accounts of Jesus' life, death, and resurrection compelling, commanding, and inspiring. They went from ordinary people like you and me to empowered people, continuing to do the teaching and miracles like Jesus had done. They did not conform to their present age but were transformed by the renewal of their minds and hearts.

The transformation of these first Christians began when they experienced the Holy Spirit descending upon them at Pentecost (Acts 2:1–12). They experienced the living presence of Jesus as he had promised before he died. His presence gave them power to do the same things that he did while he was on earth. They then had a divine worldview, which allowed them to see life differently and continue the transformation of the world in his name and by his power. These early Christians were from many different backgrounds but drew together because they served the same Jesus. They had a contagious fire in their heart, and many who saw them wanted to commit their lives to Jesus. We read in Acts 2:37–41 that there were 3,000 people who wished to join the disciples who had been filled with the Holy Spirit at Pentecost. Peter told them how they could join this divine outpouring of grace. They had to repent and be baptized. Again, we read that *metanoia*, the turning around from a mere human worldview, opened the way for them to make a total baptismal commitment to Jesus as Lord of their life. This adult decision to give their life over to God allowed them to experience the gifts of the Holy Spirit and the power to do the things that Jesus did.

Acts of the Apostles gives us a compelling picture of the power of a transformed life. We read of the many miracles that happened at the hands of those first people who committed their lives to Jesus' ministry. In my book, *Healing Miracles in Acts of the Apostles*, I described 18 miracles occurring through the ministry of people like you and me. They healed the sick, cast out demons, and raised the dead by the power of the Holy Spirit within them. That same Spirit is available to us. They received it through an adult total commitment of their lives to God with an openness to the gifts of the Holy Spirit.

This adult baptism and transformation were normal for the first 300 years of Christianity. There is evidence that the same miracles we read about in the gospels happened in the Christian community during those years. The healing ministry was a normal part of community life. There are also many stories about how these transformed people did not back away from proclaiming Jesus' message. These writings encourage us to open ourselves to all the gifts of the Holy Spirit. The retreat that we went through in chapter two can be a tool to help people experience this full, transforming power of the Holy Spirit. Churches would benefit from re-establishing an occasion when adult Christians and non-believers could be taught about the full effects of the Holy Spirit, fully surrender to Jesus as Lord of their life, and then receive prayer for the impartation of the Holy Spirit.

Another aspect of the Christian life we discover through Acts of the Apostles is the boldness with which the early leaders spoke. In Acts chapter 4, we read how angry the Jewish leaders were that Peter and John proclaimed Jesus' resurrection from the dead. They had also just healed a crippled man who they met at the temple gate (Acts 3:1–16). Even though the leaders told them to stop their preaching, Peter and John continued, "filled with the Holy Spirit." Remember, Peter and John would have been considered to have no personhood in this culture, yet they have a dynamic personhood empowered by the risen presence of Jesus within them. The Jewish leaders observed their "self-assurance" and did not know what to do with them. After being released from this interrogation, they returned to the community and shared what God was doing through them. The power of the Holy Spirit fell on the members of community again and gave them all more courage to proclaim the message of Jesus. The churches today need leaders with this kind of courage who do not compromise the gospel with the teachings of the culture but are transformed by the anointing of God's Holy Spirit.

The power of Jesus' presence shows up in full force as we read about the conversion of the apostle Paul (Acts 9:1–22). He was a Jew, and his mission was to stop the growth of the early Christian community, but Jesus stopped him in his tracks on the road to Damascus. Jesus met him there and revealed his risen presence in a way that transformed Paul and gave him a whole new worldview. He was blinded for a time so that his eyes could be opened to see life with God's eyes. He began a new life with a divine worldview. Instead of persecuting the Christian community, he began to preach the message of Jesus and grew communities in many different countries. He surrendered his life to the work of God and became a powerful instrument for proclaiming Jesus' saving message to the world. His journeys recorded in the later chapters of Acts of the Apostles show a man on fire with the Holy Spirit ready to accept any suffering to bring others to know the depth of Jesus' love. He no longer conformed to the present age but was transformed by the renewal of his mind so that he could judge what was God's will.

Acts of the Apostles also describes the great transformation that occurred in Christianity during those first decades. At first, the followers of Jesus were all Jews. Gradually, non-Jews wished to join the group, which was a significant barrier for the Jews since they were taught not to associate with Gentiles. But Peter was open to the direction and surprises of the Holy Spirit. In chapter 10 of Acts, we read how Peter broke through his human understanding and went to this Gentile's house. The Jewish Christians, to that point, considered the Gentiles unclean, but Peter received a vision from God calling him to step through these old categories. This gave Peter the courage to go to the house of Cornelius. On his arrival, he was welcomed by a large number of people who were waiting to hear him speak. Peter gave his testimony about Jesus, how he was crucified, rose from the dead three days later, and even ate with his disciples after he rose. Before he could finish, the Holy Spirit descended on the whole crowd of people who were listening, and they began speaking in tongues. With that occurrence, Peter felt that God had opened the door for Gentiles to be baptized, so he had Cornelius and his household baptized.

The same thing happened to Paul as he traveled and preached about Jesus. In chapter 15 of Acts, we read how the early Christians gathered in Jerusalem to discuss the issue of allowing Gentiles into the community. Peter, Paul, and Barnabas were there to describe the movement of God they witnessed as Gentiles were being transformed by the power of the Holy Spirit. After some discussion and discernment, the Christian leaders agreed that God was inviting Gentiles to be part of the Christian community with the understanding that they would change some of their behaviors. They were to "abstain from anything contaminated by idols, from illicit sexual union, and from the meat of strangled animals" (Acts 15:20). This major decision by the early Christians shows that they had been "transformed by the renewal of their mind." They broke out of their life-long mindset, which had them to believe that they could not relate with Gentiles. They were now welcoming Gentiles into their communities. This was a major breakthrough. Jesus had given them a new view of reality. The power of the Holy Spirit melted past cultural differences and broke down century-long divisions. Since most of us are non-Jews, this decision opened the door for us to become Christians.

The second half of Acts describes the journeys of Paul. We read about his many challenges and the unrelenting tenacity with which he continued his divine mission. His courage and acceptance of persecution are inspirational to anyone who takes Jesus' message into the world. Many people committed their lives to Jesus through his preaching, but there was almost always serious resistance from the Jews in various countries. Even after he was stoned in Lystra and dragged out of the city for dead, his disciples prayed over him. He got up and went right back into that town (Acts 14:19–23). He was not to be stopped because the divine energy of the Holy Spirit empowered him.

One last story that has always impressed me is the account of Paul and Silas in Philippi (Acts 16:16–39). When Paul and Silas were on the way to their place of prayer, they met a girl possessed by a spirit. She followed them, shouting about who he and his followers were. After several days, Paul commanded the spirit to leave, and immediately, the girl was freed from her clairvoyant spirit. That spirit was no match for the Spirit that filled Paul. The girl was set free, but her masters lost their source of profit, which they made from her. For this act of kindness, the magistrates had Paul and Silas flogged and put in prison with their feet chained to a stake. Paul and Silas spent the night in prison "praying and singing hymns to God as their fellow prisoners listened." He models for us what we can do when we are in a challenging situation. Then, an earthquake broke open the doors of the prison, and the chains came loose. The jailer thought they had all escaped and was going to kill himself because that was more honorable than getting killed by his superiors for letting the prisoners go. Paul "shouted to the jailer, 'Do not harm yourself. We are all still here.'" All the prisoners even stayed, though they were free to go. They had heard the singing and saw a miracle. After the jailer saw this miracle, he asked what he needed to do to be saved. Paul invited him and his household to believe in Jesus. He had the opportunity to teach and baptize the jailer and his whole family. Paul's ability to consistently manifest the love of Jesus, even in prison, opened the way for him to change many lives. His transformation kept him eternally connected to his Master.

The final verse of this account reveals the depth of his commitment to Jesus' mission. These verses tell us that if Paul had spoken up the night before and told the magistrates that he was a Roman citizen, he would not have gotten flogged and imprisoned. What was he thinking to remain silent? I believe Paul was not thinking but listening to the Master's voice. He could have missed the pain, but he would have missed the chance to bring the jailer and his family to salvation. He models a listening spirituality that sometimes can cause inconvenience and maybe even some pain, but doing what Jesus asks has some awesome, miraculous results.

These and many other stories in Acts portray what it means to be part of the Christian community. It is a life lived in the world but not of the world. It is a life set apart, directed and empowered by the divine Spirit. If the church of God is going to be revived, it must pull out of the present cultural trappings and the mistakes of the Middle Ages and recover its roots in the bedrock scriptures and Acts of the Apostles. It must be transformed by the renewal of its people "so that they may judge what is God's will, what is good, pleasing and perfect." Churches today, if they are going to bring about a divine transformation, may need to stop doing what they are doing and explore more closely the bedrock scriptures. They may need to take a new look at how the first disciples of Jesus received empowerment and how they listened to the voice of the Master. They may need to revive the core of Christianity and be open to the power of the Holy Spirit.

Prayer for Transformation

Jesus, I read of these early Christians who were radically changed by your Spirit. They were people like me who became courageous ministers of your message in a time when your words were not welcome. They had to hear your voice when new people came to you, and their old categories did not fit the situation. They had to break loose from worldly ideas and proclaim the new message you brought to the world. Jesus, I do not know if I could do those things, but I ask you to help me do what you need me to do in my world to change lives as they did. Give me the words to say, the actions to take, and the steps to follow to bring more people into your saving presence. Move me past my fears of change, and clearly show me where you are leading. Send forth the fullness of your Holy Spirit with all the gifts I need to carry your message into the world around me. Thank you, Jesus, because I know you will do this. Amen.

Questions

Which stories in Acts of the Apostles most inspire you?

Would you have been a member of this early Christian community? Why or why not?

If you have a church community, is it like the community in Acts of the Apostles? If not, what would need to change?

Chapter 7

A Man on Fire

We have looked at Paul's conversion and some of his travels as he told the story of Jesus and the journey to salvation. In this chapter, we will explore some of the treasures he left us in the letters he wrote to the communities he founded and visited. What he writes in these early bedrock letters is very informative to understanding the core of the Christian faith.

Paul was most responsible for taking the teachings of Jesus and translating them into a language that the Gentiles could understand. His letters are part of the bedrock scriptures and give us an understanding of how the first Christians sought to pass on the message of Jesus to the world. Paul started many Christian communities in various countries. He wrote letters to these communities with instructions about Jesus and the practices that were in keeping with what Jesus taught. He affirmed the moral teachings of Jesus (1 Corinthians 6:9–11). He promoted women's equality as Jesus had done (1 Corinthians 7:4–5). He negotiated a way for the Jews and Gentiles to get along and share in table fellowship (Galatians 2:11–14). Like Jesus, he accepted all the suffering that was part of proclaiming Jesus' message and saw his pain as beneficial for the salvation of those to whom he ministered. He also spoke boldly and never compromised Jesus' teachings to avoid pain. He spent his share of time in prison for speaking about Jesus, but even from prison, he wrote, "Rejoice in the Lord, always! I say it again, rejoice! Everyone should see how unselfish you are. The Lord is near. Dismiss all anxiety from your minds. Present your needs to God in every form of prayers and in petitions full of gratitude. Then, God's own peace, which is beyond all understanding, will stand guard over your hearts and minds in Christ Jesus" (Philippians 4:4–7).

Paul had the fire of the Holy Spirit burning in his heart. His letters are filled with statements that describe that fire and his ability to carry it with humility. He wrote, "I am the least of the apostles; in fact, because I persecuted the church of God I do not deserve the name. But by God's favor I am what I am, and this favor to me has not proved fruitless" (1 Corinthians 15:9–10). His words give us courage that even if we have failed God at times, we can still be part of his transformed people. We recognize that God's favor, God's Spirit, takes us into the world of the impossible to do things beyond our capabilities. We do not conform to the world but live in a realm of divine energy coming to us through our deep commitment to God's will. Paul gives us a picture of the power of divine obedience, of daily listening for God's instructions and moving in divine favor.

In his letter to the Galatians, Paul speaks of people who tried to alter the gospel of Jesus and make it conform to the culture. Paul writes, "We resisted this so that the truth of the gospel might survive intact for your benefit" (Galatians 2:5). His words encourage those who remain faithful to the gospel today. He continues in that letter to say that he checked his teaching with Peter, James, and John after his conversion to ensure that he was accurately teaching what Jesus had said (Galatians 2:7–10). One role of Christian leaders is to guard the truths of the gospel. Paul had a keen sense of making sure that wherever he traveled, he would speak as Jesus had spoken.

Paul also shared a unique sense of equality and the power of unity that a connection to Jesus brings. He wrote, "Each one of you is a son/daughter of God because of your faith in Christ Jesus. All of you who have been baptized into Christ have clothed yourselves with him. There does not exist among you Jew or Greek, slave or freeman, male or female. All are one in Christ Jesus" (Galatians 3:26–28). Like Jesus, he taught that people are equal in personhood, even if their roles are different. They each are called to align their behavior with what Jesus taught and love with sacrificial love as Jesus did.

Paul's life displayed a deep care for people. He was truly transformed by the renewal of his mind. He encouraged his disciples to care for each other with love. He wrote, "Your love must be sincere. Detest what is evil, cling to what is good. Love one another with the affection of brothers and sisters. Anticipate each other in showing respect. Do not grow slack, but be fervent in spirit; he whom you serve is the Lord. Rejoice in hope, be patient under trial, persevere in prayer. Look on the needs of the saints as your own; be generous in showing hospitality. Bless your persecutors; bless and do not curse them. Rejoice with those who rejoice, weep with those who weep. Have the same attitude toward all. Put away ambitious thoughts and associate with those who are lowly. Do not be wise in your own estimation. Never repay injury with injury" (Romans 12:9–17). That is a huge order, but Paul knew it was possible because of the power of the Holy Spirit. Christians can live with a divine vision because they have been infused with a divine power. Receiving that power every day makes their journey possible.

I believe his greatest challenge came when he wrote, "Bless your persecutors" and "Never repay injury with injury." Retaliation is a strong natural instinct, but our Christian witness calls us to curb that instinct by the power of God's love inside us. God did not retaliate when humans abused their free will. Instead, he absorbed the pain and effects of human sins into himself on the cross. The Christian witness of not fighting back when unjustly treated has been one of the most notable traits for non-Christians to understand. It has been this behavior that brought many to seek the message of Jesus. It is possible when we allow Jesus' love to bring inner healing and forgiveness so that our hearts are deeply connected to his heart.

In his letters, Paul makes some statements that are worth our reflection. We pondered a number of those when we made the retreat. Each shows the depth of his understanding of Jesus and the effects of his resurrection. He writes, "If the Spirit of the one who raised Jesus from the dead dwells in you, then he who raised Jesus from the dead will bring your mortal bodies to life also, through his Spirit dwelling in you" (Romans 8:11). This bedrock scripture gives us the assurance of our own resurrection to eternal life with God. It tells us that those first Christians had this belief, giving them the courage not to fear death. Paul displays that kind of courage. When we are called to make sacrifices or handle persecution, it is encouraging to remember our eternal destiny, which no one can take away.

Paul taught people of his communities that they could be intimate with God and call him "*Abba.*" He loved the people that he served. He wanted them to feel God's closeness so they could experience the fire God's love brings to their hearts. Paul prayed, "I kneel before the Father from whom every family in heaven and on earth takes its name, and I pray that he will bestow on you gifts in keeping with the riches of his glory. May he strengthen you inwardly through the working of his Spirit. May Jesus Christ dwell in your hearts through faith, and may charity be the root and foundation of your life. Thus, you will be able to grasp fully, with all the holy ones, the breadth and length and height and depth of Christ's love, and experience this love which surpasses all knowledge, so that you may attain to the fullness of God himself.

To him whose power now at work in us can do immeasurably more than we ask or imagine, to him be glory in the church and in Christ Jesus through all generations, world without end. Amen" (Ephesians 3:14–21). We can feel this prayer being prayed over us so that we might grow in a deeper understanding and experience of God's love for us. We can experience God's presence "strengthening us inwardly" and healing any inner wounds that we may carry. This gives us a boldness and security for ministry.

In his letter to the Ephesians, Paul shares his vision of worship. He sang praise to God in prison and encouraged his people to praise and thank God often. He writes, "Sing praise to the Lord with all your hearts. Give thanks to God the Father always and for everything in the name of our Lord Jesus Christ" (Ephesians 5:19–20). He was on fire with the Holy Spirit. He spent his time honoring God. I do not know if you notice, but some churches sing almost all their "worship songs" to the people present rather than to God. The lyrics do not address God or express people's praise of God. They sing to the people in the pews. That reminds me of the two men who came out of church after worship. The one said, "I didn't like the worship." The other one replied, "That is all right. We weren't worshipping you." Paul reminds us to make sure we are worshipping God and not ourselves or the people in front of the church. We do not want to conform to the culture but be transformed by the renewal of our mind.

In his letter to the Philippians, Paul quotes an old Christian hymn describing Jesus as God coming to earth as human and then being raised up again to the full prerogatives of his divinity. He left his glory above to enter our world, and when his redemptive mission was finished, he was raised and brought back to what his divinity affords him. We take a moment to soak in this early hymn. "Though Jesus was in the form of God, he did not deem equality with God something of be grasped at. Rather, he emptied himself and took the form of a slave, being born in the likeness of humans. He was known to be of human estate, and it was thus that he humbled himself, obediently accepting death, death on a cross! Because of this, God highly exalted him and bestowed on him the name above every name, so that at Jesus' name every knee must bend in the heavens, on the earth, and under the earth, and every tongue proclaim to the glory of God the Father, Jesus Christ is Lord" (Philippians 2:6–11). These words summarize Jesus' attitude and divine mission. Paul uses the hymn to call his people to humility and surrender to the Father's will. He quotes the hymn to try to give words to the mystery of Jesus coming to earth as God to redeem us. It is impossible to describe the mystery, but we can feel the gratitude and honor that Jesus deserves. This is probably the oldest writing in the New Testament, and it shows the awesome gift of Jesus coming to earth for our redemption.

Paul clearly understood the need for having deep, solid roots in faith. He wrote to his community at Colossae, "Continue, therefore, to live in Christ Jesus the Lord in the spirit in which you received him. Be rooted and built up in him, growing ever stronger in your faith, as you were taught, and overflowing with gratitude. See to it that no one deceives you through any empty, seductive philosophy that follows mere human traditions" (Colossians 2:6–8). He knew there were people who offered "seductive philosophies," which sounded somewhat good but were not what Jesus taught. This practice also goes on today. Some people teach in the name of Jesus but do not teach what he taught. As followers of Jesus, we are challenged to remain faithful, to hold on to our bedrock scriptures and our commitment to Jesus as Lord of our lives. Being renewed in mind means taking time to learn and study these scriptures and continually refresh our surrender to Jesus.

We read how Paul calls his disciple, Timothy, to stay faithful to the core teachings. He wrote, "Take as a model of sound teaching what you have heard me say, in faith and love in Christ Jesus. Guard the rich deposit of faith with the help of the Holy Spirit" (2 Timothy 1:13–14). Timothy would come up against many different philosophies in his role as leader of a community, and Paul had to ensure that he would guard the true message of Jesus as he received it. The role of the disciple is to stay faithful to the Master.

Paul summarized his instructions and the way of living the transformed life. He wrote, "Because you are God's chosen ones, holy and beloved, clothe yourselves with heartfelt mercy, with kindness, humility, meekness, and patience. Bear with one another; forgive whatever grievances you have against one another. Forgive as the Lord has forgiven you. Over all these virtues put on love, which binds the rest together and makes them perfect. Christ's peace must reign in your hearts, since as members of one body you have been called to that peace. Dedicate yourselves to thankfulness. Let the word of Christ, rich as it is, dwell in you. In wisdom made perfect, instruct and admonish one another. Sing gratefully to God from your hearts in psalms, hymns, and inspired songs. Whatever you do, whether in speech or in action, do it in the name of the Lord Jesus. Give thanks to God the Father through him" (Colossians 3:12–17).

These statements and teachings come from a man on fire for Jesus. He never backed away from doing what Jesus required. He traveled much and suffered greatly to proclaim Jesus' message. He told the Corinthian community, "We are afflicted in every way possible, but we are not crushed; full of doubts, we never despair. We are persecuted but never abandoned; we are struck down but never destroyed. Continually we carry about in our bodies the dying of Jesus, so that in our bodies the life of Jesus may also be revealed" (2 Corinthians 4:8–10). Most of us do not get treated as roughly as Paul did, but his drive to preach Jesus' message on every occasion can inspire us all. He was truly transformed by the renewal of his mind and heart.

Paul has always been an inspiration to me. Once I experienced Jesus' deep love for me, I read through all his letters and felt a man with the fire of the Holy Spirit in his heart. I have modeled my ministry on his. I have sought to proclaim Jesus' healing power and teach as he taught. I have no thought of stopping. I feel a fire in my heart that will not go out. There is a mission to be done, and nothing is more valuable than doing it. There is a message to be preached that people are longing to hear. This book is about that mission and that message. It is meant to light a fire in you, to fill you with energy and a Love that overflows from your heart to everyone you meet. It is the fire, the Love of the Holy Spirit that empowers the transformed life, the fullness of life.

Pray for the Fire of the Holy Spirit

Jesus, you called Paul to carry your message to the world of that time. You infused him with your Holy Spirit and directed him to many places to preach your word, impart your Spirit, and light the fire of your love. He faithfully carried the torch of your presence to all the places you directed him. He accepted the price of doing your mission and kept the joy of your presence in his heart. Jesus, enkindle that fire in me. Make me burn with a passion to proclaim your message to the many people who need to hear it. Help me radiate your intense love that brings healing to your people. Give me the language to draw people into a love relationship with you. Fill me with the courage to step out of my comfort zone and share the healing and saving power available to all who desire it. Give me the discernment to know which direction to go. Thank you, Jesus, because I believe these things are being done. Amen.

Questions

Which message of Paul do you find most compelling?

With what challenges in Paul's life do you identify?

Have you felt the fire of the Holy Spirit in your life? If not, would you like to?

Conclusion

What Does This Mean for Us?

We have looked at Jesus' picture of God and taken time to retreat and soak in God's deep love for us. We have noted the healing available to us through quieting ourselves and listening to the voice of Jesus. We have examined the bedrock scriptures to get an accurate account of what Jesus said and what his voice sounds like as we seek to be guided by him. This experience and knowledge change our lives and empower us to live transformed lives. Once we no longer conform to the present age but are transformed, we see things differently and act differently than the world around us. We become the salt of the earth, which gives a different flavor to the situations in which we find ourselves. Instead of seeking worldly pleasure and power, we experience the deep joy of walking daily in God's will with Jesus walking beside us. Our decision to surrender our will to God's will opens the door for the Holy Spirit to move in us, empowering us to do things beyond our human capabilities. We see the miracles that are possible because it is no longer only us doing things but divine power moving through us.

The apostle Paul used the image of earthen vessels to describe this phenomenon. He wrote, "For God, who said, 'Let light shine out of darkness,' has shone in our hearts, that we in turn might make known the glory of God shining on the face of Jesus. This treasure we possess in earthen vessels, to make clear that its surpassing power comes from God and not from us" (2 Corinthians 4:6–7). Even though we are not perfect, we recognize that we carry a perfect treasure within ourselves. We possess the creative and healing love of God. We possess Jesus' forgiveness and redemption won for us on the cross. We possess the gifts of the Holy Spirit, as Paul describes in 1 Corinthians 12:4–11. We carry the peace of Jesus which he promised us. We carry an inner joy knowing we are in union with our Creator. We can release all these things within us through our surrender to Jesus so that we can bring transformation to others.

As we take time every day to quiet ourselves and receive divine love, these things will manifest themselves more fully in our lives. This is a transformation. Even if we have known Jesus for a long time, the relationship and the power of his presence become stronger and stronger the more we surrender. If we have not known Jesus, our decision to surrender to him opens the door to receive all these treasures, which will gradually grow in us. The transformed life is filled with deep joy, and there is excitement about how God will use us next to bring new life to the world around us.

The present age needs us not to conform. The world needs people who will bring the power of God's presence into life's situations. The world needs people who will experience God's healing power and then share this great treasure. The world needs the wisdom of Jesus, which is found in the bedrock scriptures, so people can discover what behaviors are destructive to humanity and learn how to live healthy lives as Jesus intended. It needs people who have discovered the freedom of repentance and surrender to their Creator. The world needs people who listen to God's voice every day and share that voice in their communities.

The churches today need people who will not conform but "be transformed by the renewal of their mind and heart, so that they may judge what is God's will, what is good, pleasing and perfect." The churches need people who are not after human power or recognition. The churches need people who will not keep doing the same thing and watch their communities shrink away. The churches need people who will proclaim and practice Jesus' healing power. The churches need people who will teach like Jesus taught, with his authority, and not be swayed by non-Christian messages.

The churches need people who will speak about the original meaning of the Eucharist and invite everyone to make a weekly recommitment of their body and blood to Jesus, who has offered his body and blood for their redemption. The churches need people who will gently call one another to repentance, to *metanoia*, turning away from worldly practices and turning toward the One who can give them the fullness of life. The churches need people who know how to make disciples for Jesus. They need people who will bring holy, transforming revival for the benefit of all people.

Jesus needs you and me to be those people. We cannot stand by and watch people in the world destroy themselves, nor can we stand in churches that do not know the treasures available to them. We cannot keep being silent when so many spiritual lives are at stake. We must allow ourselves to be totally transformed so that our lives will make a difference for the glory of God. Be one of those people.

About the Author

Rev. Paul has spent his 47 years of priestly ministry passionately leading people in his community and surrounding area to a deep love for God, teaching about the power of God's word, and bringing God's healing touch to many. He has traveled to Australia, Europe, Guatemala, Kenya, Uganda, Madagascar, and nationally, teaching and ministering God's healing love.

Rev. Paul has written seven books:

Arise and Walk: The Christian Search for Meaning in Suffering
Paul's Letters for Today's Christian
Journey to Inner Peace
Sacraments: Encountering the Risen Lord
Resting in the Heart
Healing Miracles in Acts of the Apostles
Where Do I Come From? My True Identity

In 1979, he became an active member of the Association of Christian Therapists (www.actheals.org). He is now spiritual advisor to that community. In 1996, he became a member of the International Order of St. Luke the Physician (www.OSLToday.org), an international organization dedicated to equipping God's people with the healing ministry of Jesus. He has served as president of their board and continues to help lead their ministry. He is also on the National Board of Directors for Christian Healing Ministries (www.christianhealingmin.org), directed by Judith MacNutt.

About the Author

Rev. Paul retired eight years ago from serving as pastor of St. John's Church and Center for Inner Peace in New London, Wisconsin. He was able to initiate growth in the church by the power of the Holy Spirit to the point where they went from nearly closing to needing a new church building. He designed the new church and was the main builder for that structure. St. John's was a central place for teaching, worship, and healing ministry for his last 18 years as a pastor.

He has a fire in his heart for inviting people into the heart of God. His gifts of preaching, teaching, praying, and administrating have been anointed by the Holy Spirit to bring many people to greater wholeness and inner peace.

Books for Further Reading

Feider, Paul. *Healing Miracles in Acts of the Apostles.* Oregon: Wipf and Stock, 2021.

(This book takes the reader into eighteen of the healing stories in Acts of the Apostles to discover the power of God's love available to those who commit their lives to Jesus. It has discussion questions for group sharing.)

Feider, Paul. *The Journey to Inner Peace.* Oregon: Wipf and Stock, Revised 2015.

(This simple, experiential book offers important steps on the journey to true inner peace in Jesus. It speaks of the spiritual base for doing healing ministry. It contains practical application questions and prayers for healing.)

Feider, Paul. *Resting in the Heart.* Oregon: Wipf and Stock, 2001.

(This book offers simple, clear steps, along with scriptural reflections, to assist the reader in getting free from childhood memories that stifle their adult life, especially in the areas of fear/anxiety, shame, unresolved grief, and unnamed anger.)

Feider, Paul. *Where Do I Come From? My True Identity.* Oregon: Wipf and Stock, 2022.

(What is my true identity? How do I perceive myself? Do I have within me a deep inner joy and peace because of who I am? This unique book takes readers on a profound reflective journey to discover answers to life's most important questions, which readies them for the opportunity to bring peace and healing to others.)

Johnson, Bill. *When Heaven Invades Earth*. Pennsylvania: Destiny Image, 2005.
(A dynamic presentation of how to bring the power of heaven to the world today through the "special forces" given to you by the Holy Spirit.)

Keating, Thomas. *Intimacy with God*. New York: Crossroads Publishing, 2009.
(This is an excellent book on spirituality. It offers numerous methods for experiencing God personally. It speaks of many ways to allow God's presence to heal our inner hurts and free us from the things that keep us from feeling his deep love for us.)

Keller, Timothy. *The Prodigal God*. New York: Riverhead Trade, 2011.
(The author reflects on the story of the prodigal son and shows how both sons needed to repent of their behavior toward the generous father. He shows how the banquet is open to all willing to change and receive love.)

Keller, Timothy. *The Reason for God*. New York: Riverhead Trade, 2008
(The author answers some of the major questions people have about God by presenting a well-thought-out reason for faith in God, who loves deeply. It is a great resource for helping people talk about their faith to those who may be skeptical.)

MacNutt, Francis. *Healing*. Indiana: Ave Maria Press, 1999
(This is one of the best comprehensive books on Jesus' healing ministry and the commission we have to continue his healing work. It is an excellent resource for people learning about healing ministry.)

MacNutt, Francis. *The Healing Reawakening.* Michigan: Chosen Books,2005

(A unique account of how Jesus' healing ministry has survived through the centuries of Christianity and is viable today.).

Miller, Craig. *Breaking Emotional Barriers to Healing.* Pennsylvania: Whitaker House, 2018.

(The author offers profound insight into the connection between wounded emotions and physical illness. He offers methods to release the underlying emotions and bring about physical healing.)

Moreland, J.P. *Love Your God with All Your Mind.* Colorado: NavPress, 2012.

(Moreland makes a compelling case for Christians to use their God-given intellect to help in their spiritual development and enable them to bring others to believe in Jesus.)

Nouwen, Henri. *Life of the Beloved.* California: PublishDrive, 2002.

(This book rings with the affirmation that everyone is loved by God and can enjoy "the life of the beloved." It reveals the wonders of the spiritual journey and renews the fire of faith as much for the prayer minister as for the prayer recipient.)

Ortlund, Dane. *Gentle and Lowly.* Illinois: Crossway, 2020.

(The author uses Jesus' words about being "gentle and lowly in heart" to reflect on who he really is, especially for those weary and faltering on their life journey.)

Rice, John. *Called to Bless—Restoring God's Ministry of Blessing.* Oregon: Wipf and Stock, 2024.

(This book focuses on God's promise to bless and our calling to bless one another. Many blessing stories are interspersed throughout the book, revealing how God's goodness and grace are released when we speak words of blessing wherever needed.)

Strobel, Lee. *The Case for Christ*. Michigan: Zondervan, 1998.

(The author presents an enormous amount of evidence to show that Jesus is the Son of God and that he rose from the dead. He demonstrates the validity of Christianity.)

The Spiritual Enrichment Retreat by Rev. Paul Feider.

A **six-part video series** which helps participants experience the full release of the Holy Spirit with all the gifts of the Spirit. It contains a leader's manual and a participant booklet. It is downloadable by emailing Jamie at sharing@osltoday.org

COMMUNITIES THAT TRAIN AND SUPPORT PEOPLE IN THE HEALING MINISTRY

Christian Healing Ministries at
www.christianhealingmin.org

The International Order of St. Luke the Physician at
www.osltoday.org

The Association of Christian Therapists at
www.actheals.org